IS THERE A SPEAKER
IN THE ROOM?

For a complete list of Global Management titles, visit our website at www.goglobalmgt.com or email us at infoGME@aol.com

IS THERE A SPEAKER IN THE ROOM?

Libby Hammond
Cartoons by Alex Owens

To Dick (who has to deliver two inspirational, purposeful and practical talks every week for the same audience!), Natalie and Peter, the loves of my life, and to Dorothy, Albert, Louise, Hilary, Robin, Lucie and Julie – the best 'out-the-box' thinkers in the world!

Published in 2009 by Global Management Enterprises, LLC. Massachusetts, USA

ISBN 978-1-934747-51-3

Contents

Acknowledgements

I am delighted to thank all the wise speakers for their contributions. Particular thanks to Robin Sieger for his model of integrity and excellence as a speaker. A special thanks to Nick Richardson of Interphiz Ltd who has been so generous with his wisdom and advice; to Alex Owens for taking the plunge as my illustrator – isn't Frank great! – to Philip and Dee for reading the final copy, and finally to the Father, Son and Holy Spirit for filling my life with kindness, purpose and joy.

Foreword

I had an involuntary shaking in my left leg and, given the state of my mouth, I was wondering if I had drunk any water in the past ten days. On top of that, I had just begun to have a panic attack in conjunction with a major full-blown cold sweat.

I wasn't jumping out of a plane for the first time, I was giving a presentation to 300 people in Germany at a sales seminar. That day, I recognized the truth of the saying, 'knowledge is not power; it is applied knowledge that is true power.'

I have spoken all over the world to many diverse audiences. I have seen the best in the world, and they have one thing in common – they leave nothing to chance. They prepare and they practice to the point of mastery. They have a comprehensive knowledge of the topic and they magically can bring it to life, painting memorable images in the mind of the audience. They are passionate, and when it is all over, they practice and prepare some more.

The key is that there are, in truth, no short cuts to platform excellence. There are many dos and don'ts, and most of us learn the hard way (in my case, on a stage in Germany). This book is filled with strategic wisdom for all speakers and will accelerate your learning, your understanding, and your ability to become the best speaker you can be.

This book will give you the knowledge. The passion, preparation and practice – that's up to you.

Good luck!

Robin Sieger

Introduction

In the film 'The Paleface,' Bob Hope plays the part of Pinkerton Potter, a genteel dentist who, having landed in the Wild West, is assured that he has what it takes to fight a duel with a well-known gunfighter. After trying to steady his nerves at the bar, Pinkerton, appropriately attired for the gunfight, makes his way out of the saloon and, as he passes, groups of well-meaning cowboys, sitting at the dusty tables, ply him with helpful tips to survive the gunfight. This advice covers: how to stand at an angle to avoid the oncoming bullets, where to aim his gun, which side of the street the sun would be shining on, how to position his hat, which hand the sharpshooter would draw from and so on.

By the time he had covered the short distance from the saloon to the street for the duel, he was sweating, walking with a limp, had a crick in his neck and was so intent on remembering the advice about getting the gun out of the holster, he almost got shot by the bemused gunfighter. Happily, Pinkerton had Jayne Mansfield on his side; she shot the baddie from a hotel window ... but not everyone has a Jayne to look out for them!

Many people today are called upon to speak to audiences for a variety of reasons.

- There are the professional keynote speakers and trainers who have a clear ability to communicate important truths which can motivate and bring about change in their listeners.

- Along with keynote speakers are the After-Dinner speakers (standup comics, Burns Supper specialists, corporate dinner speakers), sporting celebrities, film and television celebrities, scientific specialists, business gurus and so on.

- Many others are thrust into public speaking as a result of their position in a company and are called upon to speak on behalf of their businesses at internal staff and external promotional events.

- Then there are the tremendous number of people who have been suggested as speakers for a local charity, Rotary Club, Chamber of Commerce, etc., because they belong to a speakers club – or often by well-meaning friends!

As director of a speakers' bureau, I provide a consultancy service specializing in providing strategic influencers for events. By strategic influencers I mean speakers and trainers who are first class communicators with first class ideas that influence the audience. In the course of my work, I meet many speakers who are at the peak of global careers, others who are tentatively exploring the whole arena of professional speaking and those who have to present to staff and clients because of their position at work. My work with clients and speakers is aimed at ensuring (a) that the client knows their event needs are fully understood, (b) that the speaker resourced will deliver to a fully researched brief and (c) that – most importantly – the desired outcomes for those in the audience will be achieved.

This book is written from the overview of a bureau working with both clients and speakers and seeks to look at the heart and attitude of speakers. I've sought to debunk and unclutter some of the mystique about presentation skills and the world of the professional speaker. This is a very practical book which aims to give the kind of wisdom and advice that will be really helpful to anyone involved in speaking to any type of audience. It is meant to encourage, challenge and refresh speakers at all levels and hopefully to stir up a passion to continue to go for excellence. It will also refresh principles for continuing on the way to excellence for those already established in the speakers' market.

We will look at, among other things; the starting point for

those considering speaking; the qualities needed to be a successful speaker; 'plates and pebbles' – preparation and content; working with bureaus; developing a business; and ... wise words from the masters and young Jedi! There's also a chapter especially written for teachers and pupils to give guidelines on the key elements of a presentation – there are many potential speakers who have their self-confidence unseated after doing their first 'show and tell' at an early stage in life!

Frank Speaker will join us along the way – you met him on the front cover having the kind of experience many a speaker will identify with. Each chapter is honest, informative and has practical steps which will be helpful for this journey of walking in the way to excellence.

'That's the difference between me and the rest of the world! Happiness isn't good enough for me! I demand euphoria!'
Calvin (Calvin and Hobbes)

1

To Speak or Not to Speak – That is the Question

It was said there were three profound truths about Christopher Columbus: when he left Spain he didn't know where he was going; when he arrived in the New World he didn't know where he was, and when he returned to the Spanish court he didn't know where he'd been! The one thing that is very clear about Columbus is that he was highly motivated, not just by the thought of bringing wealth to his country, but by the whole process of risk and adventuring into the unknown. Unrealistic expectations were brought down to earth by the hard realities of the expeditions, but, despite setbacks in getting royal patronage for his trips, he persevered, finally got his break and then totally by accident, he changes the course of world history and becomes the most famous seafarer in the world!

The great thing about the adventure of being a speaker is that, like Columbus, as long as the passion is there, the skills needed to start, travel and be the best can be learned. I can imagine Columbus as a child watching boats sail away and dreaming of wild adventures exploring the world. As with all dreams, they could only come true when, at some point, he put his foot on the deck of his ship and set sail. His raw skills were developed through experience. He matured through learning to cope with disappointment and, in the midst of everything, he retained his sense of adventure.

'The world is extremely interesting to a joyful soul!'
Alexandra Stoddard

The same principles that affected Columbus can be applied to the life of a speaker. **Motivation** is what starts you on the journey of learning to be a speaker and keeps you going when you go through lean times – facing difficult audiences and dealing with failure. **Expectations** – developing blue sky thinking, together with a positive, expectant attitude that can lead to growing speaking opportunities and improved performance. And the **realities** of living the life of a speaker – it is hard work turning dreams into reality. There are essential skills to be learned, some to do with speaking and others to do with marketing yourself, building a business as a speaker and staying fresh. Finding the right openings, learning how to get a good brief, competing with the many others who can speak on the same subject and so on, can be challenging, frustrating but ultimately immensely rewarding for those who have what it takes and are willing to persevere. It's important at this point to mention that there is a world of difference between motivation and passion, which we'll cover in a later chapter.

Let's look at these three: motivation, expectations and realities, in more depth.

Motivation, expectations and realities

For anyone involved in speaking, the crucial question is 'What is your motivation?' Why? Because it is out of what is in your heart that your mouth speaks!

In explaining to Newsweek why he'd gone to college rather than join his father as a human cannonball in the circus, Bob Kuechenberg related the following motivation for his choice. 'My father and uncle were human cannonballs at the circus and my father said I could either go to college or be a human cannonball. A few days later, my uncle shot out the cannon, missed the net and smacked into the ferris wheel. I decided to go to college.' While he had been motivated to join the circus because of family ties, the impact of his uncle's encounter with the ferris wheel brought reality into the picture, clarified his thinking, so that his motivation for going the college route communicated itself with great conviction.

The transition from someone who gives talks either within the business context or more informally to clubs and so on, to building a career as a speaker, can be precipitated by a variety of reasons. It may be that in the course of giving a talk on behalf of your company, you are 'spotted' by someone in the audience. Some time later that same person might suggest you as the perfect speaker for their business dinner or conference. You may then be asked what your fee is, or be offered a fee and eventually, you may find yourself being approached by an agent.

Another reason can be that you hear someone speak for what seems a rather large fee and you say to yourself 'I could do better than that!' It may also be that you belong to a speaking club and a time comes when the cost and time spent in traveling, preparation and delivery begin to exceed the pleasure of speaking at the event – especially when, along with an invitation to speak, the mail brings the latest phone bill!

Some speakers are in the fortunate position of having sufficient income, or if already retired, good pensions that allow the freedom to enjoy speaking, almost as a hobby, without financial worries. For most though, there comes a time when a choice has to be made between speaking on an ad hoc, un-feed basis and moving into the world of the more professional speakers platform where good laborers are worthy of their hire. As with the cannonball, this is where expectations and reality kick in and the real motivation is revealed!

When considering whether to be a feed professional speaker or not, there are some key reasons that influence such a decision. The main one can simply be financial – it is costing more to support the hobby than it is worth, so it makes sense to take something that is working well and develop a business side to it. Another reason is the message someone feels they have to bring to a wider audience – they have something significant to say and they genuinely believe it is worth hearing. A third reason, which applies to a very small number of people, is ego – they just love the power of having a bunch of people trapped in a room until they've finished speaking.

1. Motivated by money?

I can sometimes hear the rustling of wads of notes in people's minds as they consider what they would like to earn as a speaker – especially when they hear sums commanded by the highly paid speakers. Unfortunately, people who are particularly motivated by building up their bank accounts reflect that motivation when they speak – in some senses they see $ signs sitting in the delegates' seats and are very strict about keeping to their allotted time based on the principle that less is more; the less time speaking the more money per minute of delivery!

First and foremost, a speaker needs to *earn the right* to charge for his or her work. Most speakers who have gone on to do well in full-time speaking have got countless engagements under their belt where there was no fee charged so that they could get as much experience as possible. All things being equal, it is very possible to start earning money as a speaker and build up a good fee structure over a period of time, the emphasis being on 'time.'

There are wonderful stories of speakers whose unrealistic expectations of making a speedy impact on the world have been brought rapidly down to earth along with their expected fee!

At a conference for lecturers, a cocky young speaker had planned to make an instant mark as a new speaker and had been booked by the client at a high fee level. Hardly waiting to be properly introduced to the audience, he strode onto the platform and launched into his speech. His papers slipped off the podium, which put him off his stride and then he got his key points mixed up, which interrupted his flow. By the time he'd finished, he walked humbly off the stage with his head down and one member of the audience turned to another and said: 'If he'd gone up the way he came down he'd have done much better!'

His motivation to make easy money made him somewhat blind to the need to grow in the other qualities necessary for successful speaking – including coping with the unexpected.

The positive aspect of being motivated by building a financially successful business from speaking is that it can be a great drive for striving for excellence as a speaker. The desire to be a great 'product' encourages an openness to feedback, no matter how negative it might seem, and a hunger to learn from others. A speaker once said to me that 'It's not what you did to make it go wrong that counts, but what you do to make it right!'

2. Motivated by your 'message'?

I just love hearing people who are passionate about their subject, especially when it is well communicated. For all of us, the experiences we have in life become part of the fabric of our being and when we find others who have had similar experiences, we share them with one another. Often someone may have a different slant on a shared experience and that can give really helpful insight to the listener although it can also be more of a Calvin and Hobbes encounter, *'Talking with you is the sort of conversational equivalent of an out-of-body experience.'* Then, before we know it, we are being so affirmed about our insight that we can feel we have to share it with groups of people – in fact, so many people need to hear this message that we really ought to speak to the nation! At this point, there is a need to get grounded in reality.

My bureau provides experts who talk with depth, clarity and confidence on their specialist topic, rather than people who are expert talkers (those who can waffle with conviction over what can sometimes seem to be a prolonged period of time!). However, anyone who wants to learn how to develop as a speaker has to start somewhere and the right motivation will bring the right results. When asked by a reporter how he had developed such a marvelous gift of oratory, George Bernard

Shaw said 'I learned to speak as men learn to skate or cycle, by doggedly making a fool of myself until I got used to it!'

The big question for any audience is 'What can I take away from this speaker session?' For every speaker who can talk on a subject such as, for example, leadership, there are several dozen (in fact, not surprisingly, many more than that) who all speak on the same topic. It is vital therefore that what you have to say has a distinct message and a high 'take-away' value for the audience. By 'take-away' value I mean that all delegates go away with at least one thing that can be applied to their lives and bring about change at either a personal or corporate level. It doesn't have to be a Damascus road experience but it must be something concrete and measurable, regardless of how small that is, because someone has paid money for your input – and the least they can receive back is value for their investment.

The most encouraging people to ask for feedback about whether what you have to say is worth listening to are friends and family – because they don't want to upset you and won't necessarily say it like it is. The *best* people to ask for feedback are your clients – the members of the audience will be realistic and don't sign names to forms! For those who are established as speaker and trainers, the same questions apply: how good is the 'take-away' content of your current presentations? Is what you deliver distinct and fresh? – we'll come back to this later on in the book.

3. Motivated by ego?

It can be a really affirming experience to have spoken to an audience that has listened, understood and been really helped by something we have talked about. We love the sense of relief when, after having spoken, we get one person after another coming and thanking us for some aspect of the talk. It may have been an illustration which was particularly relevant, a practical tool which would be of great help or just appreciation for our having come along to talk. These are the great moments we try and remember when we get back home and discover the boiler light has gone out and there's no hot water!

We're going to look at understanding self a little later in this chapter because there are some people, thankfully not very many, for whom the position of being a speaker is worth more to them than the message they have to give and this affects the working relationship with clients, bureaus and audiences. To the client they come across as very successful, confident verging on arrogant and somewhat pernickety on details affecting their personal comfort rather than details relating to the briefing. To the bureaus they can be demanding as they won't always work to the brief.

They also are a bit like the visitor to a beach watching a man and his dog trying a new trick. 'Watch this!' said the owner of the dog, tossing a stick of wood out onto the sea. The dog immediately ran over the top of the water, fetched the stick and brought it back over the waves to the owner. The visitor shook his head in disbelief as the owner repeated this trick two or three times. Finally he asked the visitor 'What's amazing about my dog?' to which the reply came 'He can't swim, can he?'

When egos get in the way, it can stop us from the pleasure of affirming others!

Understanding yourself

I'd like to spend a bit of time on this section particularly because it is so important. As people, we are designed with five areas of personal functioning: spiritual, rational, volitional, physical and emotional (not in any order of importance!). These areas are influenced, developed, damaged, restored and healed over the years starting from the moment we are born. From time to time, we can experience the impact of the past on our present. For example, sitting in a restaurant, the aroma of cooking herbs can bring back pleasant memories of sitting in taverns overlooking the sea and warm, dry holidays. Conversely, being ignored by the waiter can trigger feelings of rejection or low self-esteem! A helpful tool in understanding some of our internal dynamics is called the 'Triangle of Insight' which simply describes three situations which happen simultaneously.

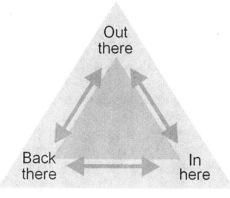

Something happens 'out there.' For example, you have started to deliver your seminar and you notice two people in the audience talking to each other and laughing. You begin to feel slightly insecure and the thought flashes through your mind that they are laughing at you. At that moment 'in here' you feel really insecure and stupid. Now you know you are very competent and good at what you have to say, but that is not what you are feeling at that particular moment. Why? Simply because 'back there' your subconscious is replaying the moment when, as a 7-year old, you presented your school project on worms to the class and two kids ruined this significant moment by giggling all the way through it. Standing in front of the audience you are really feeling like a 7 year old in a 43 year old body!

One model of understanding this process of internal interaction of the stages of our lives is Transactional Analysis (TA). Eric Berne explained that the human personality is made up of three 'ego' states which he called the Parent, Adult and Child. Each ego state has an entire system of thought, feeling and behavior from which we interact with other people. When we communicate with each other, 'transactions' take place between the different ego states. TA practitioners identify which ego states people are transacting from and by observing the process, can stop unhelpful patterns of response and build in healthy ones. This obviously facilitates very effective communication skills because not only are negative reactions being replaced with positive ones, but the 'games' played out through dysfunctional behavioral patterns are also stopped. Berne labeled some of the games people play with names like 'I'm only trying to help you,' 'Why don't you,' 'Yes but,' among others – do these ring a bell?

By recognizing that we can subconsciously make self-limiting decisions about ourselves in childhood as a survival mechanism, we free ourselves up to make healthy changes. There are some excellent books on self-understanding, and I would recommend you do some reading on the subject, e.g. *'His Image, My Image'* by Josh McDowell.

There is an African proverb which says:

> *'When there is no enemy within, the enemies outside*
> *cannot hurt you.'*

As a speaker, make the effort to gain an understanding of *who you are* as a person at a level which is more than just knowing what you like and dislike. Learn to identify your strengths and weaknesses as a person. The answer to questions such as, 'Why do I react as I do?' will give the kind of information that will enable you to develop as a speaker. Put simply, you won't have so many buttons to push and you will be sensitive to not emotionally abusing your audience.

If you talk to the most successful speakers of our time, whatever their field of expertise, they will all have one thing in common – they have learned to identify and leave their personal baggage behind and they have also gained an understanding of their personality type. Nigel Risner's book 'It's a Zoo Around Here' uses examples of lions, dolphins, monkeys and elephants to describe personality types and is very readable, although while I wouldn't mind having an elephant personality, I'm not sure if I'd like the body shape to go with it!

Personal insight into strengths, weaknesses and type is an evolutionary process which, for today's top speakers, started in earnest from the moment they set out to build a business as a speaker. It frees them to work with who they are and not get bogged down in comparing themselves with other speakers. While it is really helpful to learn, evaluate and share insights and tips with other speakers, *never* compare yourself with their style of delivery or personalities. This will only result in one of two things: you either feel much better than them which will lull you into a false sense of security about your own skills (leading to the danger of having an overinflated ego), or, you will feel less able, and seeds of self-doubt as to your success as a speaker can start to take root (leading to low self-esteem and discouragement). As someone once said 'Some days you're the dog and some days you're the hydrant!'

This is one of the main reasons why it is crucial to understand what your motive is for being a speaker. The moment you go in front of an audience of people, you are making yourself vulnerable to having who you are and what you are saying open to others' comments and it is not always the positive ego-affirming experience you would hope to have. If you know yourself though, it can be a fantastic learning opportunity where any negative feedback can be welcomed as *constructive criticism* without the speaker's self-esteem being damaged.

It involves discovering the answer to the question: 'Who am I?' because the more I learn to understand who I am, the better able I am to grow in speaking out of my strengths and compensating for my weaknesses. The result of this self-understanding communicates *authenticity, clarity* of message and *confidence* in delivery – in essence the listener engages with the speaker and an empathic relationship forms. For the audience, the person they are listening to becomes someone they can have confidence in and want to do business with.

Learning to adapt

Excellent speakers develop their skills by starting with their own raw, but well-researched material both at a personal and business level and use it as a basis for giving talks. The exposure to more objective audiences rather than friends and family can lead to constructive feedback which will boost confidence in their speaking abilities. As they gain confidence, that sense of security communicates in such a way that their professional profile is raised – and other audiences want to hear them! This positively reinforces their confidence as a speaker. It is a win-win situation: self-confidence grows and so does the business.

Life is a journey of experiences and who we are at 20 is not the person we are at 30 or 48, because each passing year brings situations that contribute to greater self-awareness. The gung-ho speaker at 25, who has got the all-singing, all-dancing Powerpoint presentation that dazzles his audience will not necessarily deliver material in the same style five months later. Why? It only takes one event where the projector goes into Star Trek mode and takes the slides 'where no man has gone before' to make the speaker decide to rely less on technology and more on verbal content.

So, what do *you* know of *your* strengths and weaknesses and *your* personality type? The answer to these questions will affect the size and type of audience you are comfortable with. Some speakers prefer to work with only high level management in small groups, others can be equally happy with an audience ranging from anywhere between ten people to two thousand! As well as helping identify your favorite size and type of audience, knowing yourself will also help you to be strategic in planning a successful development plan as a speaker.

The proverb on which my business is based is from the first part of a saying by King Solomon, found in the Bible: *'By wisdom a house is built and through understanding it is established.'* It goes on to say *'and through knowledge it is furnished with rare and valuable treasures.'* This is a beautiful picture of how our personal development enhances the business we are engaged in. It is precisely because we evolve in our personality types through life's experiences, that it is worth spending time considering what type of people we are.

This can be great fun because part of this evaluation process involves having dreams for our futures.

> *'I cannot do everything, but I will not let what I cannot do interfere with what I can do.'*
>
> Edward Hale (1822-1901)

The gift of the gab

Douglas Fairbanks Jr. was invited to give a lecture. Looking round the room he said 'I feel like a mosquito in a nudist colony. I look around and I know it's wonderful to be here, but I don't know where to begin!'

Fortunately for Mr. Fairbanks, his celebrity status, good looks and winsome smile ensured the good will of the audience. Non-verbal skills are just as important as verbal ones. Nevertheless, the ability to communicate can be learned to great effect, although at some personal cost to comfort!

When the Greek orator Demosthenes first spoke in public, he was booed off the platform. He was no Fairbanks Jr. to look at and he had a weak voice – in short, he was very unimpressive. So he determined to practice day and night. He shaved half his head so no one would invite him out, and he recited poems with pebbles in his mouth to overcome his stammer. He practiced on the beach during storms by the Aegean Sea (still with pebbles in his mouth!) to be heard over the sound of the crashing waves. On top of that, he stood under a suspended sword to train himself not to move erratically and practiced facial expressions to match his sentences.

The next time he appeared in public with another orator, he won the debate so convincingly, they went off to war!

Nowadays, loading one's mouth with pebbles and shouting over the waves may result less in audience engagement than visits to the dentist for remedial work to chipped enamel. Happily we don't need to resort to shaving heads and standing under swords as there are great voice coaches, presentation skills courses and conferences we can attend, which is a great relief!

Verbal skills

When we look at 'Plates and Pebbles' in Chapter 3 we'll cover preparation and content but, to be a professional speaker, it is essential to be clear about what constitutes good verbal skills.

1. Clarity of speech

Offer good articulation so that the audience can follow what is being said, even with strong regional dialects.

Good communication doesn't mean losing your accent, but simply ensuring that what is said can be clearly understood. This is particularly necessary when telling a funny story or witty one-liner during a keynote speech. Often the audience can miss a brilliant punchline because the speaker has rushed the crucial bit to make it seem funnier or is in stitches before he has finished telling the joke (because he thinks it hysterical). The success of Del Boy and Rodney in the TV sitcom _'Only Fools and Horses,'_ are prime examples of great accents, timing and diction.

2. Appropriate vocabulary

Avoid the Harry Truman principle of 'If you can't convince them, confuse them.'

Some of the best talks I hear are given by specialists in their fields who make what they say easy for the listener to access. Conversely, I have met delegates leaving a conference where the speaker has been the best in their field but used such specialized vocabulary (with lots of abbreviations!) that, while the talk was appreciated, the level of concentration required to keep up to speed with the speaker induced a headache!

The key to good communication is knowing who is in the audience and using the appropriate vocabulary.

> *One speaker had decided to give an overview of his talk to help take his audience with him and he started off by saying: 'I'm going to look at cross-grading multi-layered yet ethnically individualized development programs that will be a continuum for identifying the study techniques of intellectually bright individuals to facilitate their ability to work on their own.' A masterly example of the audience switch-off technique!*

As long as you know your subject and don't try speaking at an event that takes you out of your depth of experience and knowledge (unless you put in the work to take your content to that level), you should be fine. If your talk is on a subject which is new material for non-experts, you need to adapt the material accordingly. This is no reflection of an audience's intelligence. For example, as guest speaker at a Parent Teacher Association evening, talking quantum physics and quarks when all they wanted were some of the fun moments in Einstein's life won't help their fundraising! This is why the brief is such a key way of keeping the level of content right on target.

3. Pace of speech

Audiences love to feel there is something engaging about the speaker's delivery style.

It is a pleasure to listen to a relaxed communicator who keeps a good pace of delivery without fearing short pauses to let what they have said fully sink in. There are two ends to the spectrum however, those who suffer from *verbal constipation* (thinking that a slow pace means what is said is of great weight) or *verbal diarrhea* (thinking that the audience needs to hear every bit of knowledge the speaker possesses, so they deliver everything they know in one short seminar – very, very quickly).

Good pace is really important for getting the best effect from stories and using humor which we'll cover in Chapter 3.

4. Tone and volume control

Some of my favorite speakers are the ones who make great use of the *natural lilt* in their voice or have learned how to develop speaking with emphasis without going over the top. They can use tone and an appropriate increase in volume to emphasize a point without sliding into Darth Vader mode – striding about the platform with sonorous tones and an overinflated sense of importance about what they are trying to communicate. Storytelling is an essential part of delivering a talk and knowing how to use 'volume control' can make the story being related particularly memorable. The danger of excessive volume is to convince the audience that the speaker knows less about the subject than is claimed, on the basis that he or she is using the 'Argument weak – shout louder' method of delivery!

As I said earlier, with the excellent services of a voice coach, all the above skills are ones that not only can be learned but should be monitored and refreshed regularly.

Non-verbal skills

We'll look at these in more detail in Chapter 4 but I'd like to highlight one or two key skills that are essential for succeeding as a speaker.

1. Reading the audience

When I was at school, I based every English essay question on the only play I knew inside out – because it was the only play I ever used for exam questions – Macbeth. I love the part where Lady Macbeth says to her husband 'Your face, my lord, is as a book where men may read strange matters ...' because it conjured up in my imagination, hilarious Disneyesque images of Macbeth's face. Whatever was going through his mind was reflected in his facial expressions.

Reading the expressions on the faces of your audience can be unnerving as some audiences can appear to be totally 'switched off' while in reality they're having a great time. It is also good to understand the culture of the country you are in and even that particular area of the country. In Scotland for example, Glaswegians, generally speaking, are enthusiastic, have a great sense of humor and are quite open about expressing how they feel by laughing or spontaneously clapping, so it is easy for a good speaker to positively engage with them. Edinburgh audiences, again generally speaking, are more formal in expressing their appreciation of a speaker and more aware of who else is in the audience, so they are less likely to engage in witty banter with the speaker at the Q&A session! This is the same on a global scale, so when you speak in other geographical areas both locally, nationally and internationally, take time to identify the main cultural traits of that place.

Statistically, 2% of an audience will love the speaker no matter what he or she does or says, 2% will hate the speaker and the other 96% are happy to go either way! Feedback forms will always reflect these three areas, and it is relatively easy to identify those members of the audience who give the negative feedback – they sometimes look like they sucked on lemons before they came into the seminar, and are often the first to make a statement at the Q&A session rather than ask a question. Likewise the positive feedback delegates are the first to come and shake your hand and buy your book!

It is important to understand why people come to hear a speaker as this helps reading their body language and is an invaluable help in keeping you on your toes. I should at this point also add in another statistic highlighted by a Gallup Poll in 1999. This showed that 17% of employees are actively engaged in their company, 67% are at work but not engaged and the remaining 16% are disengaged. This means that when a conference is put on for staff, the speaker has to accomplish something that the company has not managed to do – actively engage and bond with the audience – and do that with the 2:2:96 love:hate:ambivalence statistic going on at the same time!

> *'The positive thinker sees the invisible, feels the intangible,*
> *and achieves the impossible.'*   Anon

So what are some of the reasons people come to hear you speak and what attitudes will they engender?

- They have been told to attend by their boss – *possible resentment or attention-seeking.*

- It's a pleasant way of being out the office for a half day or day – *relaxed, open but possibly easily 'switched off.'*

- It is almost time for the annual appraisal and they need to show they're actively developing their skills – *open but anxious.*

- They genuinely want to learn something new and helpful – *open and keen.*

- They may have to give a presentation themselves on a similar topic and are there to 'borrow' some, or in some cases, a lot, of your material – *'switched on,' studious and taking copious notes!*

- They may also have an axe to grind. These are the type that just can't wait to use the Q & A session as a platform for their own issues – *mildly/moderately aggressive, obtuse and mostly closed.*

To be able to 'read' the audience involves getting a feel for where they are 'at' before you start to talk, while you are talking and how they seem at the end. Just as a speaker has non-verbal communication with the audience through how they stand, move, facial expressions and eye contact, so too the audience communicates non-verbally with the speaker and each other. This is primarily through body language: looking at watches, heads resting on hands and bodies sliding into snooze position are quite common in the session after lunch! This is the dreaded 'graveyard' slot and can be very challenging to even the most professional of speakers – the more courses for lunch the greater the challenge.

> *A normally enthusiastic speaker related the frustration she felt when addressing an accountants' conference after a particularly splendid lunch. Several members of the audience started to show clear signs of postprandial snoozery and no amount of animated gestures, raised volume or snappy delivery could keep them awake. She resisted the temptation to go over and call them out as part of the role-play and was glad that the session was a short one.*

It is thought that the average concentration span for a listener is about five to ten minutes. The longer the speech, the harder it is for the audience to concentrate on what is being said. However, I should say that this doesn't necessarily have to be the case – how many of you have sat through three hours of Lord of the Rings: The Fellowship of the Ring and felt the time had flown by!

2 . Body language

How someone enters the stage, moves or doesn't move during the talk, and how he leaves, all communicate to the audience what the speaker feels about himself. The first impression the audience gets of the speaker happens the minute the first step is taken on the platform. This sets the tone for what happens next.

- **The Indiana Jones entry onto the platform** – bounding on with great speed and a sense of urgency – conveys confidence and energy and can either make the audience slightly nervous as to what is going to come next or expectant that something good is coming next.

- **Nervousness** can turn an inexperienced speaker into an instant standup comedian with all the gestures but not the command of jokes required to capture the audience. Conversely, they can become very controlled and too dry-mouthed to give the initial three-minute introduction the 'WOW' factor it was meant to have. It can also create the wrong impression of who you really are as a speaker and what you have to give.

'Our remedies oft in ourselves do lie, which we ascribe to Heaven.'
William Shakespeare, *'All's Well That Ends Well'*

- **Walking confidently on to the platform** with an engaging smile to both the person who has introduced you and to the audience is a key means of bonding with the delegates.

  Eric Erikson, the psychologist, stated that there were seven stages of development in people and the very first one, which is from the point of birth to one year, has to do with bonding and trust. When the mother smiles at the newborn baby, a bonding takes place which, as this continues, enables trust to be built, and the baby feels safe, secure and learns to smile back. Trust is established between the deliverer of all good things (warmth, food, clean nappies) and the recipient (who has to do very little in return except smile, dribble and produce products for the clean nappies!). When we come on stage and smile, in a sense we are, in a subconscious way, recreating the bonding moment and communicating that we can be trusted.

Secrets of success – Jack and the beanstalk

A camper van pulled into a campsite and three children leapt out and began rushing about setting up the tent, unloading gear and, while the boys set up the table and chairs, the girls and their mother got the food cooking. A nearby camper was amazed and spoke to the father: 'What an example of teamwork.' To which the father replied, 'Not at all, we just have an arrangement that no one gets to go to the toilet until the camp is ready.'

The hard part of getting started is not getting booked for speaking engagements but in doing the preparatory foundational work. If you imagine that being a speaker is a bit like a Jack and the Beanstalk experience, you will understand one of the secrets of success. When Jack climbed the beanstalk and got into the giant's house, he had to climb a set of stairs. He looked up and it seemed too difficult but he got up the first step, then the second and so on until he stopped to draw breath. At this point, he turns to look down the stairs and is amazed and impressed at how far he has come, until he turns round and realizes he still has quite a way to go! However, the key is not to get discouraged but to *enjoy the step you are on* until you are ready to tackle the next challenge.

1. A mentor

Jack would most probably have benefited from having a mentor to talk him through the process, someone else who had already dealt with giants and beanstalks! The right kind of mentor can be immensely helpful – someone who has experience in speaking, is professional in his or her approach and has the qualities we'll be looking at in the next chapter. There is nothing more encouraging than being able to get pre-emptive advice which saves you making unnecessary and simple mistakes. Whether you are starting out or have been a speaker for a few years, it is immensely helpful to have a role model, someone you respect and have a relaxed relationship with.

A young composer visited Mozart to get advice on how to develop his talent and was told to start with simple songs. The young composer complained about writing simple songs when Mozart, as a child, was already composing symphonies. 'That's very true,' replied Mozart, 'but then I didn't need any advice on how to develop my talent!'

A healthy mentoring relationship is challenging, non-judgmental and very constructive with no sense of competitiveness. Unhealthy mentoring tends to leave the one being mentored with a sense of being controlled and feeling very insecure. Three principles in recognizing unhealthy mentoring are:

- **Misplaced loyalty** – 'I alone know what is right for you' which can make you feel disloyal if you take someone else's advice above your mentors.

- **Scare tactics** – 'You'll go down the tube if you don't take my advice.'

- **Humiliation** – the mentor publicly ridicules his or her protégées when they step out of line in such a way that it is difficult to put your finger on whether it is a joke or in earnest

Happily these cases are not very common but, forewarned is forearmed!

At the end of this chapter, as with each chapter, is a practical checklist that will be particularly helpful when worked through with a mentor.

2. A game plan

> *The man who removes a mountain*
> *begins by carrying away small stones.*
> Chinese proverb

Jack had a game plan: today giant beans, next we climb, then we take the strong man's treasure! Beanstalks aside, setting goals each year will ensure that you achieve your aims to develop and stay successful as a speaker. These goals should be very *practical, achievable* and *timetabled*. It is a wonderful thing to say you have a goal to be a world class guru on genetics within three years. However, when your actual field of expertise is after-dinner speaking as a sporting commentator you may have to question whether this goal is achievable –

unless you plan to do a degree in genetics!

Goal setting needs to cover areas such as:

- the number of fed or unfed speaking engagements aimed for in one year
- staged development of the business, e.g. web site, biographical material, branding, finances
- skills development using mentor, coach, attending conferences etc
- personal development – working with strengths and weaknesses
- expanding range, depth and freshness of material
- raising your profile, e.g. networking with bureaus and other speakers, joining the Professional Speakers Association, etc.
- paperwork – setting up contracts, procedures for working with clients and bureaus, and especially vital – a good filing system!

It is always harder to work on those goal areas that we don't particularly enjoy. For some people, it is easy to work at their publicity material and web site rather than setting up an efficient filing or bookkeeping system. For others, phoning possible clients and networking is what they excel in, but lose all the bits of paper they write contact details on – and here we can learn something from the raccoon and the giant panda! The giant panda focuses on eating bamboo. It loves bamboo and nothing else gives it as much pleasure to eat. The raccoon on the other hand will eat whatever it needs, some more and some less pleasant, taste-wise, than others, but necessary for survival. Guess which species is growing in numbers and which is fighting extinction!

3. Feedback, evaluation and re-evaluation

A question for those who have been speaking for more than

several years – where are you aiming for over the next three years at a personal and business level? Are you setting goals that stretch you out of your comfort zone? Are you keeping up to date with others who are speaking in your field of expertise and ensuring your material is fresh and your delivery different from what it was one year ago? Develop your own evaluation sheet and don't worry about what is negative or positive, simply keep focused on your goals and use feedback as a course correction.

I should say that one of the beautiful things about spending time on the question of 'Who am I?' is that negative feedback is less likely to affect your self-esteem. Rather, it will be a means of objectively assessing what should be improved in either your content or delivery. Positive feedback will be warmly received but, with a secure sense of self, won't give you an overinflated ego!

Two Texans were boasting about the size of their ranches and the first, when asked about the name of his ranch said it was called the Lazy Z, Circling C, Simple 4, High Chapparal Mountain Fountain. The second rancher was amazed and asked how many cattle he had. 'Not too many. Very few can survive being branded!'

Be encouraged and have fun

_'Before the beginning of great brilliance, there must be chaos.
Before a brilliant person begins something great,
he must look foolish in the crowd.'_
I Ching

The most important thing is to remember that if you take on board the principles in this book, there is no reason why you won't go on to become one of the top speakers and, if you are there already, stay there. Focus on what you are aiming for and don't get discouraged when things don't go to plan because the future comes one day at a time!

'The greatest oak was once a little nut who held his ground.'
Unknown

Practical checklist for little acorns and mighty oaks

Look at the following checklist and select two that you need to work on immediately, prioritise the rest and aim to have worked through them all systematically.

✍ Define your motive.

✍ Who is or could be your mentor?

✍ What are your strengths.

✍ What are your weaknesses?

✍ What is your personality type?

✍ Check out the content of your talks for 'distinctiveness'.

Who else is saying the same thing?
How long have you been saying the same thing?
What would make your content distinct?

✍ Evaluate the 'takeaway' element for the audience.

If you were sitting in your own talk what would you take away from it?

✍ Identify changes that have taken place in your professional development.

What has helped you to stay 'fresh'?

✍ Identify your 'triggers' - how have you dealt with them?

✍ Feedback sheet (Appendix 1) Use a comprehensive feedback sheet to get objective reactions to your abilities as a speaker - friends are great but they won't necessarily tell it as it is.

It may seem a lot to think through but remember, only Robinson Crusoe had everything done by Friday!

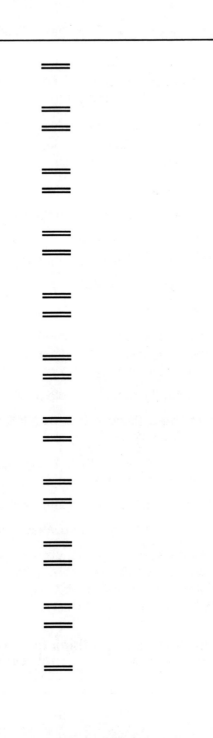

2

The 'Q' Factor

'Many a man's reputation would not know his character if they met on the street.'
Elbert Hubbard (1856-1915)

While James Bond has his 'M,' a figure of power and authority who sends our intrepid spy off to dangerous assignments (all accompanied by fantastic special effects and unlimited resources), speakers have their 'Q' – qualities of character and professionalism that minimize dangerous assignments, relying less on gadgetry and more on superb skills! In the other chapters, we will look at all the practical elements of preparation and content along with building a business but in this chapter we're going to concentrate on the qualities that make a speaker stand out from the crowd.

Integrity of character

You are the advert for your product which is – yourself! As with any product, the purchaser needs to know that the product can be relied upon to do what it claims to do – in short, it can be trusted. As Anthony de Mello said, *'If you talk the talk, you'd better walk the walk.'* Speaker integrity is vital in building good relationships with clients, bureaus and the audience and once a pattern of integrity has been established, it becomes easy to maintain. What do I mean by speaker integrity? It is very simple, you need to be consistent in how you *walk the talk.*

Walking the talk

1. Building trust

The story is told of a tourist who walked too near to the edge of the Grand Canyon and, losing his footing, slipped over the edge but was saved from plunging to his death by his fabric camera strap which, having got caught on a rocky outcrop, was now starting to fray rapidly. As he was yelling desperately for help, a calm, authoritative voice from above said, 'I can help.' Relieved, the stricken tourist called up 'How are you going to save me?' and the reply came, 'Let go of your camera strap and have faith.' There was a stunned silence and the tourist yelled, 'Is there anyone else up there?'

The first contact a client will have with the speaker can often be by phone either after a bureau has made the booking or directly with the speaker him- or herself, and remember, *first impressions always count*. There can be a variety of reasons why the speaker has been contacted; someone heard him speak and recommended him, another speaker suggested him, he was on the radio, a bureau recommended him or the speaker did some telesales on his own behalf and so on. No matter how well established or famous you are as a speaker, for the client or the bureau, if they haven't used you before, *you are an unknown quantity*. All they will know of you will have come from someone else's recommendation – even if they have heard you speak before, others in their team may not.

It is not uncommon for speakers to have their 'lemon' moments when for whatever reason, at one particular event – usually when they've had a fantastic introduction with the best showcase audience they could wish for – they do or say something totally out of character and it leaves everyone, including the speaker, slightly (or in some cases, extremely) taken aback.

The story goes of one speaker whose wife went away for a short break and he decided to give her a surprise and tidy the house. Under the bed, he discovered a small box with $1000 and 3 eggs which perplexed him and when his wife arrived home, delighted to see how he'd made the effort to prepare a meal and tidy the house, he asked her about the box. She told him that every time he got negative feedback, she'd put an egg in the box. He was impressed to think there were only three eggs in the box so he then went on to ask her about the $1000. That was simply explained, she told him – every time she got a dozen eggs she sold them!

There are some very simple tools which can help communicate that you can be trusted.

- Remember the client's name and correct business title.

- Phone when you say you'll phone, and return calls speedily.

- Professional excellence in your paperwork – this doesn't mean you can't use recycled paper but it does mean no spelling mistakes or poor grammar which rings alarm bells for the client if you're the keynote speaker!

- Listening to the brief and asking intelligent questions.
- Keeping fee integrity – which we'll come to later.
- Being proactive in serving the event's organizer – they aren't always aware of the logistical needs of a speaker, so where required, help them think through your needs, e.g. accommodation, dietary needs, PowerPoint and technical support, travel arrangements and water on the podium.
- That you're fit for the client's audience is far more important than fee!

In short, as Mark Twain said, *'Let us endeavor so to live that when we come to die, even the undertaker will be sorry!'*

2. Setting boundaries

Boundaries are a great way of helping to set standards of consistency. They protect a speaker from getting into difficult situations with clients and bureaus, and they help a speaker stay focused on developing their own standards of excellence in content and performance.

Imagine you are in your own field – a field with a boundary wall around it. There are three things a good boundary wall can help achieve.

1   It prevents you from yielding to the temptation of distraction. Often when we see something elsewhere, the temptation is to get side-tracked and we climb over our wall and work in someone else's field while ours goes to weed.

2   It protects us by stopping others from coming in and distracting us from what we are doing or, in some cases, stealing or damaging our crops.

3   It gives us a means of measuring our achievements – we can work creatively on developing different parts of the field.

Translating this into setting boundaries as a speaker, here is a checklist of areas that you need to think through and then include in your wall:

- **What type of clients** would you want to keep or avoid, e.g. is it cost effective to work with ones you have to drag your fee out of over a very long period? They may eventually pay their fee but does the hassle and anxiety involved outweigh the end fee?

- **What type of bureaus/agents** would you want to work with or avoid, e.g. does it bother you what the end client is being charged if it involves adding unacceptable markups to the client (one speaker discovered the client was charged $10,000 but his fee for the event was $3,000!). Remember it is your name they associate with the high fee, not the bureau's.

- **What number of events** will you do either for no fee or a reduced fee (charity or showcase) per year? This helps keep you focused on building your business and at the same time makes your contribution to the charitable sector much more meaningful to you.

- **Work/life balance** – does your work always take priority over planning your holidays or do you take regular time off so that you stay fresh and enjoy life – and if you're married, protect family life. No-one's epitaph ever read, *'He wished he'd spent more time at the office.'*

Fee integrity

One of the big dilemmas for a speaker can be what fee to charge and how to increase it ethically (well I hope ethics come into it!). If a speaker is established in business with a good record of experience and speaking within his or her industry, then I usually ask what the consultancy fee would be and that then becomes the basis of the fee schedule. In order to raise your profile as a speaker, it is good to do a number of unfeed speaking engagements and we'll look at that later in the book when we talk about how to build your business. If your starting fee is your consultancy fee, then thereafter you would have to consider what audience feedback you are getting. The better the feedback, the greater the 'takeaway' element for the audience and therefore the value for money for the client.

Each year you can incrementally raise your fee, for example, by between $200 – $500 (and in some cases more), but this really has to be reflected in the quality of service you provide to the client. However, once you set a fee, you must stick to it – one speaker who usually charged $1,500 was told the client budget was $5,000, so they charged $5,000. But at a conference, two clients met, one who had paid $1,500 and the other who had paid the higher fee. It doesn't take too much thinking to guess which one felt cheated and what impression was left with both of them about the speaker's integrity. It's also important to be realistic about what fees the market can bear and some of the highest feed speakers will be more successful in one part of the world than another simply because one market can pay their fees while another can't.

If you are going to reduce your fee in order to take a booking, make clear to the client that your normal fee is, for example, $2,000 but you are willing to reduce it because:

a) you have a special interest in this particular audience

b) there is the promise of other work with that particular company and this is a goodwill 'taster' – (ensure you get this in writing as a contract so that the client has to pay you if future work doesn't arise from your 'taster' session).

c) the fee is to go to your favorite charity

d) you know the organizers and this is a special favor to them.

These are just a few reasons, but they give an idea of how to maintain fee integrity without jeopardizing potential bookings.

I said at the start of this section that one of the big dilemmas

can be setting the fee schedule. However, another dilemma –
and this is for the bureaus – is the speaker who never changes
his fee. I have been faced with the situation where clients have
turned down using a speaker, who is about the best in the field,
simply because the client couldn't believe they were as good as
their promotional material said they were. One positive result
however was that another excellent speaker had to raise his
very low fee to an appropriate level and got the booking – the
client was delighted and the speaker took his wife on holiday!

Three keys on fee integrity:

- be realistic
- be consistent
- be value for money.

Money is marvelous but it isn't everything so be careful not to
compromise your reputation for integrity by compromising your
fee integrity.

*When John D Rockefeller's accountant was asked how
much he'd left after he died, the accountant to probably
one of the wealthiest men in the world replied 'Everything!'*

Authenticity

> *'It is not true, as some writers assume in their treatises on rhetoric, that the personal goodness revealed by the speaker contributes nothing to his power of persuasion; on the contrary, his character may almost be called the most effective means of persuasion he possesses.'*
>
> Aristotle

This picks up on what we talked about in chapter one on understanding who you are and being true to yourself. Audiences, generally speaking, can sense very quickly whether a speaker and their message are the genuine article and that adds real authenticity for the audience – in short, the listener feels that what is being said rings true.

When you try to *create* an impression, that is exactly the impression you create and audiences don't like it, react to it and will switch off. We'll look at using other people's material in the next chapter but, as far as possible, use your own experiences and stories from life and work to flesh out your talks. When you share a funny story, you will genuinely be amused by it and so will the audience, and when you illustrate a particular point by using an appropriate personal story, the listener's empathy will be genuine. Another thing is not to be afraid of being honest – one of the things that the business world in particular needs are speakers who will say what needs to be said – in the best possible taste of course!

At a business conference, Nicky du Preez, editor of Atlanta magazine was asked by a member of the audience what she would do to motivate three members of her staff. Nicky's reply was simple – let them go! Nicky then went on to explain that if someone is always complaining and they are not happy in their job, no matter what was done to accommodate them, then they would demotivate and wear out those around them. It was not the answer the questioner expected but Nicky's gracious honesty was genuinely appreciated.

I want to add a cautionary note here for events organizers. There are occasionally speakers and trainers who have very little experience in the business world but know how to word their publicity material to sound as if they are the genuine thing. Their aim is to 'con their way' onto a platform with a very different agenda and ultimately recruit lots of clients who will pay for their services. Fortunately, the more switched-on audience members can identify something which isn't as it should be but others in the audience may not be so astute. For the event organizer, the depth of content will not match up to the brief. When we cover marketing later on in the book, I'll highlight some pointers for reading between the lines.

Professionalism

The brief

The brief is crucial to preparation and content, which we'll cover in Chapter 3. So what is a brief and what do you need to do to ensure the brief is as clear as possible?

Basically a brief covers four elements for an event:

- the client's desired outcomes
- the audience needs
- the length and content of the speaker's contribution
- logistics, i.e. technical requirements, who to contact, travel, accommodation and so on.

A full sample questionnaire is found at the end of the book (Appendix 2) which should be very useful – and you can add or change it to suit your specific purposes. What we'll look at are some key tools in obtaining the best brief.

1. Company culture

Where practicable, meet the client and before you do so find out about the company they represent. (You can go on the Internet or whatever, but be as intelligently informed as you can without going over the top about it). There is no substitute for a face-to-face meeting as it gives a real feel for the client's personality and vice versa. It also allows an opportunity to get a feel for the culture of the company or organization hosting the event.

If the client is too far away, then plan to spend time on the phone when you can give them your full concentration and be able to ask the kind of questions necessary to covering all the pieces of information you'll need, not only to prepare the talk, but practical matters as well. If the booking comes through a bureau or agent, then you should still talk to the client direct and any good bureau will facilitate that after they have obtained the initial brief.

Once the brief is obtained, keep in touch with the client and be available to them so that any tweaking can be made prior to the event. A really good spin-off from this level of contact is that it builds a good rapport with the client prior to the event which in turn makes everything slightly less stressed.

Bearing in mind that some clients can be really difficult to work with (demanding all sorts of extras for no added cost, not returning calls, giving the wrong information in response to questions, booking you into the cheapest flea-pit they can find etc), professionalism is the quality that will motivate you to rise above it all – and never work for that client again!

2. Intelligent listening

Listening is a bit like completing a jigsaw puzzle: the client will give the broad picture but there will be gaps, and by listening well, you will spot the gaps and ask the questions which will supply the information to fill the spaces. I often find that clients have a perception of what they need, in terms of speaker or trainer resource, that is somewhat different from the *real* need – what the audience wants.

For example, one client wanted to book a high-powered motivational speaker to get their staff enthused about selling the company product. As we talked through the audience, their past history, what challenges they were facing and so on, it became obvious that what they really needed was a scenario expert to give them an understanding of the financial context in which they were working and the mindset of their potential clients. The result was that we used a scenario expert who left the audience intelligently informed about their work and, while they didn't leave the room highly motivated, they were coping better with their work demands six months later – and then they called in the motivational speaker to keep them going! Confucius said, *'Knowledge without thought is labor lost, thought without knowledge is perilous,'* and when obtaining a brief, he is so right.

The most important people at the end of the day are the audience and so the section of the briefing which deals with 'desired outcomes' is crucial. Obtain measurable outcomes from the client. When preparing the talk, these specifics act like a lighthouse which will keep you focused on preparing your talk around the client's brief rather than straying off course. At the end of the book is a sample questionnaire (Appendix 2) which you might find helpful in pre-event briefings and, in talking with other speakers, you'll get lots of other ideas.

3. Work to the brief

Imagine the scene – the client is explaining that they want you to address the subject of communication skills and the brief outcomes reflect that. You've just been to a personal development conference on NLP (Neuro Linguistic Programming) and it's now your hot subject. You've worked some (in fact a lot) of new material on NLP into your communication pebble (next chapter!). It was a bit tricky but you managed it. Now here is the temptation! The client really wants communication skills for their call centre staff but you'd love to give them pure NLP. The answer to this dilemma is very simple – don't! Please avoid using someone's event as a platform for your personal speaking agenda as, apart from anything else, it won't do your reputation any good and there is nothing worse that earning the title of 'prima donna!'

4. Keeping records

This is why you need a really good office set-up as no matter how good email and phone calls are, you must keep a record of conversations, emails and correspondence – all in hard copy in a file. We've all had experiences of little bits of crucial information jotted on little bits of paper that mysteriously disappear. Emails are fine to store until your machine crashes and, if not backed up, are lost in the ether. Whatever you carry in your head will, like the proverbial Chinese whisper, get muddled over time between what has been stored in the brain and what is eventually put on the file if not written down straight away. The venue can get mixed up, the time, who you're to meet and so on. Discipline yourself to stick to good office procedures and alongside this maintain a record of expenses, remembering to retain receipts for invoicing later. We'll look more into this in Chapter 5 on building your business.

Courtesy

One of the things that gives me greatest pleasure in being around some of the best speakers is their courtesy to those around them. From the doorman at the hotel entrance or the waiter bring extra coffee, to the technicians behind the scenes, all are treated with the same courtesy and respect by the speaker. The speaker gives them his full attention when he or she expresses thanks for whatever they have done and it's just great – and what goes around comes around.

A speaker at a prestigious hotel helped the waiter clear the table by passing over plates when he didn't need to, opened the door for him to get through to the kitchen and gave him a generous tip. A few weeks later, a large booking came through from this hotel chain – the waiter was the owner having some 'back to basics' experience!

Be a learner

After winning a playwriting contest, twelve writers were given a year's fellowship money to train, study, produce, write, act and attend lots of seminars. Two of the playwrights took their money, wandered off and wrote on the basis of people they met, places they visited and in general absorbed what was going on around them. At the end of the year, the two playwrights who became famous were the two who wandered off – Tennessee Williams and Arthur Miller!

When you have a teachable heart and your mind is open to learning, then there is no limit to how you can continue to develop and hone your skills as a speaker. Meet with other speakers, read good books, take on board client feedback but also *observe life*. If you don't do so already, why not keep a journal of interesting encounters or observations about people, along with good quotes, anecdotal stories and so on, which will add to the content of your talks.

> *'Ability is what you are capable of doing.*
> *Motivation determines what you do.*
> *Attitude determines how well you do it.'*
>
> Lou Holtz

Enjoy receiving affirmation

One of the drawbacks of the British culture is that we don't appreciate success either for ourselves or others in the way other cultures would. For example, the Americans are great 'can-do' people – and when someone achieves some measure of success, no matter how small, it is always affirmed. We need to grow in both giving and receiving positive affirmation.

Practical checklist

1. What boundaries need to be set or have been broken and need to be re-established?
   - with Clients
   - with bureaus
   - work/life balance
   - with fee integrity

2. Your fee schedule - is it:
   - realistic
   - consistent
   - value for money

3. How thorough is your briefing?
   - understanding the company
   - understanding desired outcomes
   - audience details
   - technical details

4. How would you rate your:
   - courtesy
   - integrity
   - attitude to learning

   How would others rate them?

3

'Plates and Pebbles'

The opera singer Mary Garden always motivated herself with one thought before she went on stage. She would look at the audience from the wings and think of the one person in the auditorium who had scraped together the money to come and hear her perform, then she committed herself to giving that one person the most passionate performance of her life.

A motivational speaker is simply someone who is passionate about something which is close to their heart. *That's* what makes them very motivating to listen to.

The plate

Imagine you are looking at a big wooden plate which has beautiful pebbles sitting on it. The 'something' we've just talked about is what I call the 'plate' and defines the thing that a speaker is passionate about. Anything sitting on that plate is connected to it and the plate supports anything that rests on it. Most people don't spend time defining what they are passionate about but it is really important to do so because there is, as I mentioned in Chapter 1, a significant difference between motivation and passion.

When asked what it means to be a motivational speaker, Robin Sieger, replied *'I'm not a motivational speaker, I'm passionate about people and that's my motivation.'* Whether talking on leadership, change, communication skills or whatever, a true passion for people permeates all of Robin's talks and that touches the audience, leaving them inspired and motivated.

Eating your words

There's a verse in the Old Testament book of Jeremiah that says, *'When your words came, I ate them; they were my joy and my heart's delight ...'* The effect of motivation is to encourage and influence the listener to eat (take in) the words we speak. The effect of passion in delivery of these words is to catch their hearts. Passion is something which always engages the audience at an emotional level. The mind responds to truth and the heart responds to vision.

Passion pitfalls

True passion gives reality, power and authenticity to creative speech. It is important to flag up that, while emotion is an essential factor in delivering a talk, we need to avoid the passion pitfalls that can easily result in an inexperienced speaker's loss of dignity and credibility in the eyes of the audience. Even experienced speakers can also fall into these pitfalls, especially if external circumstances, for example jet lag, leave them somewhat pooped before speaking at the end of a very long evening!

I know that probably all of you would never fall into these pitfalls but, since we're looking at passion, we might as well look at what to avoid.

1 **Too intense** – this is where the speaker's body language (taut and gesturing pointedly at members of the audience) combined with stressed breathing (long sentences rushed out with gasps of breath to enable the speaker to carry on in full flight), totally wears out the audience. The speaker comes across as fanatical, and the audience feel trapped.

> *'A fanatic is one who can't change his mind*
> *and won't change the subject.'*
>
> Churchill

2 **Too personal** – using inappropriate material to illustrate the subject matter. The speaker's platform is not an opportunity

to indulge in self-help therapy. At a ladies' lunch, the speaker was wanting to encourage the audience to have confidence in themselves and, rather than keeping the talk objective, motivational and practical, she brought out a picture of herself as a little girl huddling in the corner of a room. The speaker talked personally about dealing with rejection and some of her own childhood experiences, not perceiving that she had touched 'triggers' in some of the audience. At least one delegate had to go for counseling and some others were disturbed at being used almost as therapists for the speaker. If the emotional content is inappropriately personal, the audience can feel uncomfortable and abused.

3 **Too gushy** – adding extra pzazz into illustrating point after point with excessive use of PowerPoint or props just detracts from the talk and sounds like the speaker is starting to waffle. The audience is left unclear about the speaker's authenticity.

> *'There's nothing worse than a sharp image*
> *of a fuzzy concept.'*
>
> Ansel Adams

4 **Too verbose** – this refers to assaulting the audience with a barrage of words, concepts, facts and figures when one excellent PowerPoint picture can speak volumes. The best place for extraneous material is on handouts.

Rather than listing statistics about the effects of absenteeism, stress-related illness and workloads to a conference of head teachers, the speaker, Mark Mawer, simply put on the screen a photograph of a donkey suspended in mid-air between the shafts of its cart because the weight of what it was pulling had 'see-sawed' it up in the air. Not only did it illustrate his point, but the release of laughter helped relax the audience and ensured that Mark had their attention for the rest of the seminar.

Another danger from saying too much is that in the multitude of words, you can lose the impact of your message. The secret of good delivery is to say the right things in the right way and leave the rest unsaid.

Naming your plate

When I ask speakers what their plate is, they almost always tell me what subjects they speak on, for example:

- communication skills
- leadership
- managing change
- teamwork
- marketing ... and so on.

Since they are very enthusiastic at speaking on that subject, they presume this is what I am looking for as an example of their passion.

When questioned further, they realize that while they love their subject, their real passion is something which reflects their genuine concern for people in a specific way. It may be a desire that each member of the audience understands their significance, potential, value, or, that by the end of the session some practical action step will be applied to bring about change in a delegate's life. It is really important to understand this as, when motivation (influence on the mind) is tied in with passion (influence on the heart), the result is fantastic for both speaker and audience – the clients are also very happy at the value for money aspect too!

Just as the plate supports the pebbles so also our passion supports and permeates the subject we are speaking on.

My passion is encouraging people to realize their cup is half full rather than half empty, that no matter how difficult a situation is, there will always be something good in the middle of it all that can give hope and vision for the future. Whether I speak to groups or one-to-one, my focus is on the topic I am talking on – for example, planning and preparation for a talk. However, people will often comment afterwards on how they left the talk encouraged and motivated – which is not normally what planning and preparation tends to leave people feeling. Rather, my body language, smile, use of humor and positive language is what influenced their minds with a positive message and affected their hearts. They left practically equipped and felt refreshed. I'm just happy it all went well!

Choosing your pebbles

On the 'plate' are various 'pebbles' which represent the subject matter a speaker can talk on, for example leadership or managing change, and if we took a cross-section of a pebble we would see the different layers that have added together to form the pebble. When a speaker identifies their passion (big plate), that passion as I said earlier, will permeate quite naturally, through every subject (pebble) they speak on.

Most speakers consider that they only have one or two pebbles to speak on as their specialty, but the reality is that they have several. Let me give you an example. If we take the pebble named 'leadership,' what layers might you expect to find under such a subject title? Let's take some possible layers:

1. vision
2. effective teamwork
3. communication
4. goal-setting
5. conflict resolution
6. creative thinking.

However, if I were to say let's take each of these layers as pebbles in their own right, we then reveal a much wider area of expertise for the speaker. For example:

Pebble 1 – Vision

Areas that could be covered: Communication
Goal-setting
Creative thinking
Significance
Applying change and so on

Pebble 2 – Effective teamwork

Areas that could be covered: Conflict resolution
Communication (verbal and non-verbal)
Vision
Creative thinking
Goal-setting and so on

Pebble 3 – Communication

Areas that could be covered: Transactional Analysis
Significance
Body language – Verbal and non-verbal
Conflict resolution
Use of humor and so on

I have really just cursorily gone through these pebble layers but you can see that when we begin to explore one pebble in depth, the reality is we are dealing with layers that can form pebbles in their own right. The beauty of identifying the pebbles and their layers is that the number of key subjects a speaker can talk on expands from one or two, to several – providing they do the research and work needed to develop the layers in the pebbles.

This is the real work of preparation, leading to quality content for a speaker. When preparing to meet the client's requirements outlined in the briefing paper, rather than overdosing the audience with all the information from one pebble, a skilled speaker selects one or two layers from various 'pebbles' to tailor the talk to meet the audience needs.

If you have a mainly training background but do speak or are wanting to develop as a speaker who can supply training, a major shift has to take place in relation to what *content* you include in your seminars. If you normally spend anything from half a day to two days delivering a leadership training program, the temptation is to try and take the key elements of that course and include it in your keynote. This is one of the main reasons most trainers find it hard to switch to keynote speaking – they have more material than they need and find it hard to select what is best for the audience. I've seen seasoned speakers with training backgrounds run over time because they were trying to cram in just one more thing that they felt the audience needed to hear. When we look at marketing, we can see how this can be put to good use.

Planning, preparation and content – otherwise known as:

How to guarantee a safe landing

'If at first you don't succeed, so much for skydiving.'

When it comes to preparing for a talk, there is no substitute for hard work and a well-prepared brief. The speaker that prepares well and matches his content to the desired briefing outcomes will always land safely. So assuming you've prepared your pebbles, let's look at getting that safe landing.

Planning and preparation

In the previous chapter, we looked at obtaining the best briefing and working to the desired outcomes for both the audience and the client. Good planning and preparation is more than just getting a good brief. As Wilbur Wright said, *'It is possible to fly without motors, but not without knowledge and skill'!*

1. Understand audience expectations

It is very helpful to understand what the audience is looking for and audiences have three key expectations:

- Firstly, they want to be intelligently entertained and that means leaving the seminar, dinner, conference or whatever, with a high 'feel good' factor.

- Secondly, they want some nugget of information, no matter how small, that they will remember for weeks and months ahead – it may be a joke, a wise word, a practical application for their daily lives or even the freebie video thrown into the audience by the speaker!

- Thirdly, they want to think that they could meet the best business contact of their lives, possibly leading to a new client, being head-hunted or having doors opened to a new circle of contacts.

However, when clients and bureaus plan an event, these thoughts will not be as high on their priority list as their own expectations. Clients are wanting staff motivated to work harder, become dynamic sales people overnight, or one of the most common expectations held by clients is that the speaker will achieve in one hour what several years of training and persuasion have failed to do. Understanding audience expectations enables the speaker to include content that helps meet these expectations while influencing the audience to buy in to the key aims of the brief. In so doing, a safe landing, i.e. great audience feedback, is more or less guaranteed.

Along with their expectations, audiences have pet hates:

- not being able to clearly hear what the speaker is saying
- the session running over its allotted time
- being bored
- irritating mannerisms
- being blasted with slides crammed with too much information.

It is sometimes easier to prepare a good talk bearing the pet hates in mind as it keeps the content and delivery audience-centered.

2. Avoid presumption

During a conference breakout group, a heavy-duty speaker saw one of the delegates lounging in the hotel foyer reading a paper. Without any ado, he walked up to him and, refunding him the registration fee, told him to leave as he was obviously getting nothing out of the sessions. The speaker then turned to the hotel manager who had been watching and said: 'Which company was that man with?' to which the manager replied, 'He's not with any company – he was a courier for the hotel!'

When preparing the content of your talk for a specific event, avoid the mistake of presuming that you don't need to come with a fresh mind to the event, just because you know the subject matter well or have spoken to that type of audience before. Take opportunities to talk to delegates before an event so that you can gain an understanding of what people are feeling in relation to life and work. Simple questions of the *who*, *what* and *why* variety are all that is needed, for example, who is the person you are talking to? (name), what do they do? (position and sphere of influence), why is this event of particular use to them? (reveals internal dynamics), and so on. During the event, be alert to audience dynamics and after the event obtain some audience feedback from delegates so that when you receive feedback from the client, you will also have a fair idea yourself of how things went.

3. Know your subject – and more

> *'Beware the man of one book.'*
>
> St Thomas Aquinas

Have you ever had the experience of going to a shop to buy something needed for the car engine or a particular washer for a plumbing job and having stopped the first assistant, you embark down the 'Mastermind' route of question and answer. Describing the washer you need and producing the sound effects your cistern makes resulting from the missing item are all to no avail. The assistant knows screws and nails and that's it. What relief when someone with more knowledge and experience not only gives the answer but also throws in advice on how to sort out an electrical problem you have too.

I know this might sound like common sense because, if you love your subject, you will do this automatically. However, keep abreast of the latest information on and around your subject and it will save you from embarrassment. The following 'facts' given during a history test highlight just what level of application had been put into preparing for it. Some pupils were not quite the experts they felt themselves to be.

! Moses led the Hebrew slaves to the Red Sea where they made unleavened bread, which is bread made without any ingredients. Moses went up on Mount Cyanide to get the ten commandments. He died before he ever reached Canada.

! Socrates was a famous Greek teacher who went around

giving people advice. They killed him. Socrates died from an overdose of wedlock. After his death his career suffered a dramatic decline!

! Julius Caeser extinguished himself on the battlefields of Gaul. The Ides of March murdered him because they thought he was going to be made king. Dying, he gasped out: 'Tee hee, Brutus.'

Read new material to find out what is currently being said that is useful or questionable as someone in the audience may well ask you about it. Find out what is being talked about on a global level – the Internet is very useful – and talk with others you can learn from. A useful tip is to remember that it's okay not to have all the answers. We'll look at handling tricky Q & A sessions in the next chapter.

4. Write your own introduction

The best way to ensure that you get off to a good start with your audience is to write exactly what you want the person introducing you to say. Once you're happy with what you have, this can be used time and time again with slight tweaking, as and when appropriate. There are a variety of reasons for this:

● It keeps you in control by creating the kind of introduction that prepares the audience to hear what you have to say. If you're going to talk on leadership but the introduction covers your academic or career CV and ends up telling the audience how you spend your holidays, they'll wonder why you're talking to them in the first place.

● It protects you from being the butt of inappropriate witticisms (meant to be funny one-liners but in reality they miss the mark and fall flat), about your past career or whatever.

One speaker with a very descriptive biography had selected sentences read out with relish especially the ones stating how dynamic she was. This was followed by the person introducing her turning to the audience and saying 'Well let's see if she can live up to that then.' A psychological gauntlet had been well and truly laid down and the speaker struggled to feel any motivation for the rest of the session.

- It reminds you of who you are and what you've come to say. When you're feeling nervous, hearing someone remind you of what you've accomplished is a helpful tool in settling nerves.

- You never get a second chance to make a first impression and the introduction sets the tone for this first impression.

- For people who may have heard you before, it provides a sense of familiarity and continuity.

When you write your own intro, remember the following points:

- Keep it snappy – if it is long-winded the audience will switch off.

- An intro is to help you *engage* with the audience so avoid using too many superlatives, records of achievements and long client lists.

- Include a recent personal or business achievement, e.g. just climbed K2 or recently voted the best business speaker.

- Describe the real you – don't make claims about what your talk will do for the audience, just what your passion and vision are.

- Keep it upbeat and humorous

I remember going to hear a particularly good speaker who was speaking to an audience of financial advisers. They had been in a windowless room all morning and had spent their time working out how to increase sales, meet new targets, face staff cuts and not lose their jobs – they were not happy chickens. The platform area was very small and there was little room for movement as some of the senior staff were sitting on it. The chairman introducing the speaker stood up and said; 'I want to introduce you to the most successful motivational speaker you will ever hear. He is dynamic, inspirational and you will never be the same after this fantastic talk ...'

At this point the body language in the room said it all,. They slouched in their seats, heads went down, legs stretched out with ankles crossed, shirtsleeves rolled up and arms crossed and all very tight-lipped. Basically it was 'well here's one audience you won't win over!.'

This particular speaker had once said to me 'There is no such thing as a bad audience, only a bad speaker' so I was intrigued and slightly apprehensive about what would happen next.

The speaker got up, went straight to the platform, turned to the audience smiling and said. 'Well that's the worst introduction I've ever had – you must be thinking who does this guy think he is ...' and as he skillfully started to engage the audience I watched heads lift up, arms uncross and muscles relax. From then on it just got better and better but only because he'd read the audience and was experienced enough to know how to turn the audience around.

Still planning and preparation – structure

You've got the briefing and you've also written out your introduction, so now we need to look at how to structure a *good outline* for the talk – we'll look at content further on – and as with most things in life the KISS (keep it simple stupid) approach is the best!

1. Beginnings, middles and endings

Like any great work of art or piece of literature, the first stroke or sentence is always the hardest and this can be true of formulating the 'great beginning.'

A great beginning

Simply put, a great beginning has two stages: stage one is the *introduction*, stage two *signposts* where your talk is going and flags up that an active *response* will be sought at the end of the session. Stage one only requires three minutes and two ingredients. At this point I'll quote from Robin Sieger as he is regarded as one of the finest exponents in the UK of this initial part of the talk.

> *'The first three minutes is when the audience will form their lasting impression of you. It is therefore the time that the speaker and the audience get to check each other out. In short, if the speaker is on top of his subject and has energy and confidence, that will more often than not give the audience confidence and allow them to relax, listen and enjoy as well as learn. It will also, very importantly, start the process of influencing the audience to buy in to the message – feelings have been engaged and this sets the stage for the middle section.*
>
> *'No two audiences are exactly the same and it is important that the first three minutes settles both the speaker and the audience. It also enables them to know they are in a safe pair of hands and that what is about to follow will be first class.*
>
> *'I have worked at events where the audience were allowed to spend two hours in a bar prior to coming for a pre-dinner talk that was at the last minute postponed to an after-dinner talk. The audience will never know that, so you must have confidence in the first three minutes, because if you lose confidence in yourself, you can be sure the audience will too.'*

What does this mean in practice? Simply that your opening three minutes will combine elements of verbal and non-verbal language that settle both yourself and the audience and will contain the following two ingredients.

- Thank your host for the invitation and introduction.

- Offer a really short, humorous personal anecdote, a story perhaps taken from a newspaper or magazine, or an engaging quotation that relates to the subject you are going to speak on.

This leads straight into stage two.

- **Signpost** what you're going to focus on so that the audience understands where you're going. If they know where you're going, they can buy in to what you are saying and will engage stage by stage with where you are taking them. It also assures them that you know where you're going too!

- **Highlight** the fact that you will offer them a challenge at the end – it might be to change an attitude or lift their game, but there will be something which will require a *response*.

Once you have worked on this first part of your talk, it should remain the same, with minor alterations, for as long as possible irrespective of how many talks you give – and there are seriously good reasons for this.

Firstly, it means that as you are delivering these first three minutes, you can be on *auto-pilot* in terms of the content which, as Robin says, gives an opportunity to read the audience from the platform as opposed to the wings.

Secondly, if something goes wrong technically, for example the lap mike doesn't work or the PowerPoint doesn't kick in or whatever, you can *maintain the momentum* and impact created from the point when your host introduced you and you stepped on the platform to speak.

Thirdly, it enables you to *calm* whatever butterflies that are trying to grab your attention and *concentrate* on really enjoying being there.

Like the story about Bob Hope in the introduction, I'd rather you concentrate on the simple elements of your first three minutes than give you lots of advice about what not to do. The former is much more effective than the latter but to be on the safe side, I've put a checklist of what to avoid at the end of the chapter. Focusing on honing the content of your great beginning will prevent you from making mistakes; you won't tell a long-winded joke when you've allowed 30 seconds to deliver the humorous element in your first three minutes!

A middle with a high point

If you look at the content of an ad on television, you'll notice that the product is introduced on the screen with little, if any, preamble. But our attention is on the backdrop against which the product is seen only after the scene is set for its arrival – whether by desperately thirsty soldiers back from the war looking for something other than wine, or glamorous girls throwing their long, shiny hair over their shoulders! The main part of the ad is given over to keeping us emotionally engaged with the product and, almost as an aside, what the product *does* is slipped in. The final part tells us where/how to get the product – and the sooner the better! All we know is we must *(feeling)* get whatever it is, and we justify the expense because it cleans *(fact)* the toilet better than any other product on the market *(it must if the house on television was transformed into an alpine cottage as a result of using it!)*.

So, in terms of structure, the key elements of the middle section should be emotionally engaging, intelligently informative and guaranteed to inspire the listeners to buy into the ending of the talk. This is crucial in ensuring they take something away from the session.

What does this mean in terms of planning and preparation? It means that you can use a combination of both verbal and non-verbal techniques to create the atmosphere that enables the audience to engage with your message.

- use of a PowerPoint picture/statement
- signature story
- use of quotes and jokes
- facts and figures (where strategic and relevant)
- moving about the platform or standing still

- tone of voice and use of pauses
- body language – facial, upper body, hand movement.

Signature stories and the art of storytelling

I'd like to look at signature stories and the art of storytelling. To quote again from Robin:

> 'The purpose is of a signature story is a key part of preparing to meet the brief. It is used to create a unique quality to your talk, and the signature story becomes your 'take away' long after the conference is finished, it is the thing that people will remember. A signature story should, I believe, contain the essence of your talk: it should contain the wisdom, experience and learning point of what you are on the platform to say.
>
> 'I now have a number of signature stories which can take anything from two to twenty minutes to tell. I use them according to the audience needs and the key message I have been asked to deliver. A signature story should come from personal experience and, to be truly memorable, it should be told in the first person.'

Signature stories involve the wonderful art of storytelling and are most effective when the speaker is:

- aware of how the story is impacting the listeners and reflecting that back through his own body language

- knows how to use the story's elements to make the point

- uses timing and pauses to get maximum effect from the key point

- uses the story to lead the listeners into the next stage of the talk.

Storytelling involves using information that is interesting and relates to situations, events or people that the audience can relate to.

When talking to a group of employees who were facing possible redundancy and a key outcome in the brief was that the employees would be prepared to face unpleasant news, the speaker in question introduced the following story early in the session:

A businesswoman had gone away for a few days and had asked her sister to look after her very precious cat. Her sister was not a cat lover but agreed to do it. When she returned from her trip, she phoned her sister to arrange to get the cat, only to be told, quite abruptly, that the cat had died. Naturally the cat's owner was very upset and after a few days, called her sister back and said, 'You could have broken the news in a gentler way and told me the cat was chasing a bird up a tree, had hurt itself, and then a day or so later told me it was a serious injury so that when I came to get the cat, you could have said it had passed away. Anyhow, how's mum?' The sister paused for a moment and replied, 'She's just chased a bird up a tree.'

The staff laughed and it enabled the speaker to help them face the reality of the redundancies but to see it as a means of entering a positive stage of change rather than something hopeless.

The best stories are ones that the speaker has come across either through personal experience, talking with other people or reading something which has struck a chord. The secret is to use the right story for the right audience, so invest in good books and magazines. Watch films and documentaries that can provide good illustrations and it will pay dividends.

'If you think education is expensive, try ignorance!'
Peter Drucker

As I said in Chapter 1, any personal material used should be appropriate for the event brief, but good stories that helpfully illustrate and emphasize specific points in your talk can be incredibly powerful, and coming from authentic experience, will really help the message to be remembered along with the messenger.

Just preparing what you are going to say is a lot of work and so it's really worth having a session with one of the many excellent presentation skills coaches around. They are brilliant at working on body language, voice skills, moving on the stage and so on which leaves you free to concentrate on your message. The financial investment will more than be repaid in giving you continued confidence in your platform performance

A snappy ending

One of the pitfalls of entering the final part of your talk is the temptation to repeat much of what was said earlier to ensure the audience has understood the main points.

The key element of the ending is to provide the *springboard to action* for the delegates. It should be a call to act, to apply something at a personal or corporate level which is practical and achievable. The brief outcomes should be reflected in this element of the talk.

One way of knowing if you have succeeded is from the client and audience feedback. However, it can also be some months later when you might hear of someone who was profoundly impacted by your talk and probably through a third party.

When I was meeting a client to go through an event briefing, I mentioned a Masterclass I was organizing later in the year and who the keynote speaker would be. The client then told me that he had heard the same speaker almost a year before and it had changed the direction of his life, from being careful about what he did to having an adventurous approach to his career. He was spotted by his employers and promoted. This man was really empowered in a way that the speaker would never have known from a feedback sheet. Happily I could pass that on!

Still more planning and preparation – putting pen to paper

Whether you prefer to type straight onto a computer, mind map and then write the talk, or sit with pen and paper, it is best to write out the speech in full, especially if you are not used to giving many talks. After you have it written out, you can highlight key phrases and headings and, with practice, you can reduce this to a small card with key points which you can take onto the platform.

A speaker told me that when he first started out he spent about forty hours in total preparing for his first talk with pages and pages of notes and a kaleidoscope of color from the pens used to highlight phrases and important points. He knows his subject inside out and now is much more experienced but will still take several hours checking his content against the brief and keeps notes on cards for prompting, should he need it.

A really useful tip in dealing with nerves – which we'll come to later – is to write in bold, bright print at the top of each card, words that will keep you focused, for example, Slow down – Breathe – Relax – Enjoy, or whatever is most helpful to you.

Quotes, jokes and humor

There is a real art to telling jokes and some people have it while others don't! Jokes need to be relevant, easy to follow, short and snappy or highly engaging, have good pauses for effect, be non-offensive, lend themselves to using tone of voice, and have a really good punchline. Here is one of my favorites (especially with appropriate gestures to describe what is happening).

A man goes to the pictures to watch a very intellectual French film. As he is sitting in the cinema a dog comes and sits beside him and, at the sad parts, the dog sits with tears running down its muzzle. At the funny bits, the dog sits shaking with laughter. The man is amazed and at the end of the film, he follows the dog out of the cinema, along the road until he comes to a house. He watches the dog go up to the door, ring the bell, the door opens and the dog goes in. The man goes over to the house, rings the bell and when the door opens says to the woman, 'I must apologize but do you know this dog watched a very intellectual film and it cried at the sad bits and laughed at the funny bits.' The woman replied, 'That's amazing – because he didn't like the book!'

After dinner speaking is the main arena for using jokes, one-liners and humorous stories and is a specialist field of speaking. There are many people who are asked to speak after a dinner and while they may be good at speaking, they are not true after-dinner speakers – if the audience is expecting a riot of laughter, they will be sadly disappointed. The question a speaker has to ask himself is whether the client wants an informative and light-hearted anecdotal speech, or a stand-up comic routine. If the answer is that they want lots of laughs, then leave it to the experts. Dave Wolfe, for example, is an excellent stand up comedian and excels at after-dinner events. Robbie Glen, ex-governor of Barlinnie, is not a stand-up comedian but he is superb in delivering one-liners and hilarious stories and, like Dave, will produce the same results for the client – audiences with tears of laughter running down their faces. The event is remembered for all the right reasons. Both Dave and Robbie give some excellent advice later in the book.

One of the real skills needed for after dinner speaking is handling an audience often well-oiled from pre-dinner drinks and unlimited wine. If the event runs late, the after dinner speaker can often be invited to take the floor well after 10:30pm (especially if other people are talking before the guest speaker). That may not sound too late to many of you reading this, but I'm pumpkin material after 10pm – my coach would have had to come well before midnight!

For those who haven't got the delivery skills required for telling a series of jokes, the next best thing is using really good quotes which can be genuinely funny in themselves and at the same time help make your point. Don't try and make examples fit in if they really don't as it just won't sound right. Here is a sample of what I mean (taken from real scripts!).

- *Shots rang out as shots are wont to do.*

- *The plan was simple, like my brother Phil. But unlike Phil, this plan just might work.*

- *Her hair glistened in the rain like nose hair after a sneeze.*

- *She grew on him like she was a colony of E Coli and he was room-temperature British beef.*

- *McMurphy fell 12 stories, hitting the pavement like a paper bag filled with vegetable soup.*

- *The hailstones leaped from the pavement, just like maggots when you fry them in hot grease.*

- *His thoughts tumbled in his head, making and breaking alliances like underpants in a tumble dryer.*

There are loads of resources for good quotes and facts on web sites and libraries to add to your growing resource folder. Another great resource is watching the timing and material on TV or old Laurel and Hardy films, Bob Newhart and, our family favorite, the Goon Shows!

Use humor positively. There is a place for making fun of a situation but it's not appropriate to use sarcasm, innuendo or negative humor to run either yourself or someone else down. Picking on a member of the audience to be a volunteer for something which will make them a bit of a laughing stock, is only a useful tool when the end result makes them look really good. Also not a good idea is using supposedly humorous phrases which reflect a wobbly self-esteem on your part, for example, *'I'm not exactly the best speaker in the world'* or *'I'm glad to be asked and hope I'm worth the money you paid for me'* and so on. It may be meant to make people laugh and invite audience empathy, but the reality is it undermines your credibility as a speaker, especially when you are meant to be the expert.

Platform plagiarism

> *'They copied all they could follow,*
> *but they couldn't copy my mind,*
> *so I left them sweating and stealing*
> *a year and a half behind.'*
>
> Rudyard Kipling

One of the things I love in my work is finding people who have fresh and exciting material – and some well established speakers fall into this category because they have the integrity to ensure that their material is up-to-date. There are also the next generation of speakers who have harnessed new ideas and are challenging businesses to think and act differently. In terms of content, however, I really want to encourage you to avoid platform plagiarism. There is nothing worse than listening to a speaker when you know that he is regurgitating someone else's material – sometimes almost verbatim – and passing it off as his own. The trouble with this is that these kinds of talks tend to contain errors which the listener notices.

The other obvious plagiarists are those who don't have a truly experienced business background but have cobbled some good jargon together and charge anything from $60 – $120 for the privilege of a phone call or hourly session.

This is one of the other dangers of being motivated by money as a speaker. You can see the business world as an easy market place to make a quick profit. And what quicker way of doing that than taking someone else's hard work, repacking it to look like your own and then charging a high fee. The bottom line is that clients and delegates are people with needs, hopes, fear and joys. In today's culture, there are those who seek to tap into those feelings to create a money-generating dependency on the speaker. Happily, it doesn't take too long before this kind of manipulation reveals itself for what it is and the delegates will be much wiser, if slightly out of pocket, next time round.

One of the reasons it can be hard for a speaker or trainer to stand out from the many others doing the same is simply because a client who has had their fingers burned by an inept but expensive life coach, will think long and hard before using another one. There is absolutely nothing wrong with using someone else's illustration, model or quotes so long as they are attributed to the person who originated them – giving credit where it is due.

What Howard Aiken said is also true. *'Don't worry about people stealing your ideas. If your ideas are any good, you'll have to ram them down people's throats!'*

Practical Checklist

Plates and pebbles

1 Identify your passion, i.e. your 'big plate'.

2 Identify the 'pebbles' sitting on that plate.

3 For experienced speakers, how fresh is your passion?

Content and preparation

1 How up-to-date is your material?

2 Which of the following areas do you need to work on:

- Introduction
- Beginning   - use of the first three minutes
  - signposting
- Middle
- Ending   - take-away application for audience
- Use of signature stories
- Building a resource file of stories, quotes and facts

4

'The Speaker Now Approaching the Platform ...'

'In theory there is no difference between theory and practice. But, in practice, there is.'

The day has arrived and you've arrived at the venue for your presentation, and regardless of your speaking experience, you may be feeling somewhat overtaken by circumstance ...

*... a bit like the volunteer firefighters called in to deal with an oil storage blaze which experts had failed to manage. The fire was so intense the professionals couldn't get near to the storage containers and as a last resort, they called in the local volunteer firemen. A short time later an ancient fire engine shot past the waiting firefighters and stopped a few feet away from the fire. The volunteers jumped out, doused themselves in water and went straight in to tackle the blaze which was successfully put out. The company chiefs were overawed by the bravery of these men and presented them with a big check at a ceremony a few days later. When asked by the CEO what he would use the money for, the senior volunteer replied 'The first thing I'm going to do is get the brakes on that ***** fire engine repaired!'*

When it comes to walking onto the platform, we can feel like the volunteers facing a huge blaze – we may have set out with a sense of control but by the time we arrive on the platform it feels like the brakes have failed!

First things first – checking the venue

There are some very simple practical steps to checking the venue before you go on to speak and I've added a checklist at the end. Remember the golden rule that what can go wrong very often does and while plates and pebbles are under your control, many other things aren't. So, you've arrived at the venue and, if you're staying overnight, you have dropped your bag and stuff in your room. What do you need to check and why?

The room where the event is being held

The room: Is it big or small? Is it warm enough or too cool? Is the air fresh or fuggy?

Lighting: If it is a daytime talk, are there windows in the room? Is there a lot of natural light? How bright is the electric lighting – and any dodgy light bulbs (e.g. intermittent flickering)?

Seating: Is the audience going to be near you or stretched to the back of the room? Are the chairs comfortable and well spaced for leg room?

Acoustics: Is the type of room one that deadens sound or enhances it?

Platform: Do you have room to move about (if that is your style)? Are you elevated above the audience or on the same floor level?

Is there a lectern? Is it the right height and in the right place?

Are there any potential hazards that could trip you up e.g. cables?

Technical: Are PowerPoint, flipchart and microphone available? If the microphone is fixed, is it at the right height and angle?

Who is the key technical contact? If you sent PowerPoint slides ahead, have they arrived safely and work in the machine provided? Is there a notice about switching off mobile phones?

Contacts: Who is responsible for your brief and who is the link person for ensuring you are where you need to be at the right time? Have you met the person introducing you to the audience? Who else do you need to meet, e.g. company executives, chairperson, etc?

The answers to these questions are all common sense. If the room is large and acoustically flat, you have to work harder at pauses, voice tone and volume – that can be accommodated by a good sound check to ensure that you will be heard clearly by everyone in the room. Conversely, if it is a small room with a smaller audience, you may be better with no microphone at all. The audience need to be comfortable so if it gets too warm or isn't warm enough, they will be distracted by discomfort. Most places now are non-smoking, but if the room was used by smokers during the interval, near the kitchen or simply full of sweaty bodies on a hot day, the air will be stale. A quick blast of fresh air will do the trick.

Lighting is really important – I remember hosting a showcase for speakers in Glasgow in a super marquee at the City Inn right beside the Clyde with boats sailing past. The sun was shining and all was well in the world, until we tried using the PowerPoint. The screen couldn't be seen with the bright natural daylight but, like real pros, the speakers carried on as if nothing had happened – fortunately we'd had the presentation printed off for handouts anyway.

Another thing worth mentioning about lighting is that bright electric lights combined with bright natural light can give people headaches, so if the room is bright with natural light, switch off the electric ones – you can put it down to being environmentally minded! If the lighting it on the dim side, whether because there is a video to watch or it is just poor lighting, that is when tired delegates will be tempted to snooze off.

Lighting is also important if the event is being videoed – at a *Presenting to Influence* Masterclass I was running, the keynote speaker was being videoed and the chandelier above him started to fade then come on full power. We switched the light off in the end but by then the video was unusable.

Seating that is comfortable, with generous legroom and wide aisles, makes for a relaxed audience who can take sitting through a one-hour seminar without being distracted by NB (numb bum), sore backs or cramp.

Checking out the room layout also affects audience interaction and, if you like audience participation, you may need to adjust what you've planned if the seating is not what you'd envisaged. For example, if you want people to get into groups of three or four to do an exercise but the chairs are locked together, it will be uncomfortable for those having to crane their necks or twist round to join in.

Platform hazards need to be checked out, so make sure you are aware of any cables or potential hazards, such as a wobbly lectern or a flipchart that may have been wrongly positioned, for example, in front of the PowerPoint screen. Make sure there is a glass of water out of sight but near to hand. It may also be that the spot the organizer has chosen for the speaker to be is not the best place – for example, in front of a window so that the audience has to screw up their eyes against the daylight. Familiarize yourself with where things are positioned and then you only have to concentrate on what you have to say.

Technical things like microphones, PowerPoint, audio/video systems are wonderful when they work smoothly but I can understand why more and more speakers use less and less technology. I remember one hilarious occasion when the speaker started his PowerPoint slides to illustrate his point and discovered there was a 14 second delay between when he clicked the remote control for the slide and it actually appearing on the screen. He had to continually calculate 14 seconds worth of talk back from the point he would introduce the next slide and had major brain fatigue by the time the session ended!

'Technological progress has merely provided us with more efficient means for going backwards.'
Aldous Huxley

Introduce yourself to the **technicians** and have a thorough sound check as much in advance as is necessary to run through everything. As mentioned earlier in the book, one pet hate of an audience is not being able to hear the speaker properly. We've all been to weddings where the best man, who may have written the best speech on the planet, doesn't speak loudly enough. Those sitting nearest to these gems of humor are in stitches while those at tables out of earshot spend most of their time asking the person next to them, 'What did he say?.'

Always be prepared for a worst case scenario, for example a power failure or the PowerPoint projector or computer blowing up. In that way, you avoid being technology-dependent for your presentation and are able to deliver what you had prepared in a wonderfully professional manner with or without electricity!

Contacts are vital. As part of the brief, you will have spoken to the person who booked you for the event and, if the booking came directly from the client, they will be the first point of contact at the event. If the booking came through a bureau, they will have given you those details as part of the brief.

It is important to make a note of who is in the program before and after you and have a short chat with them, even if it's just the person introducing you and whoever is giving a word of thanks. This helps get a feel for how things are going on the day and also helps a sense of journeying with this particular company team even if just for a short while.

Your brief *should* also mention the briefs given to speakers before and after you, if any. You can then ensure that your material will not overlap. Ideally, speak with these people to exchange ideas and guarantee that there will be no duplication.

Next – calming your nerves

The briefing has been thoroughly researched, the preparation has been made and you're about to deliver your content. You're standing with a bad case of vultures in your stomach – the butterflies left long ago and the introduction has been made. Your mouth is dry, you're wishing you were somewhere else and then you start to walk onto the platform. You start to thank your host when you discover your tongue has stuck to the roof of your mouth. When you try to work up some saliva you realize you'd forgotten to check if there was a glass of water by the lectern. You look up and the audience are all watching you through 3-D glasses … then you wake up!

Everyone gets nervous before standing in front of an audience – Sir Laurence Olivier was physically sick before almost every performance – and it has nothing to do with courage versus fear. 40% of a survey group of 3,000 people stated that the thing they feared more than anything else (and I presume that included war, famine, plague or whatever), was having to stand up and speak in front of an audience.

Napoleon considered Marshall Ney to be the bravest man he'd ever encountered. On the morning of what was to be one of the biggest battles Ney had to fight, he had difficulty getting into the saddle because his knees were shaking so much. When he had finally mounted his charge, he looked at his knees and spoke unsympathetically to them, 'Shake away knees, but you'd shake worse than that if you knew where I was taking you.'

We don't have to mount a horse to be aware of shaking knees, or to find that our heart is beating extremely loudly and cactus has started sprouting on our tongue to join the vultures in our stomachs! We are all familiar with the basic biology of *fight-or-flight* syndrome, where going into a challenging situation causes the adrenalin rush that makes us ready to leap into the arena (with panache and decorum of course!).

The time of waiting prior to going on to speak is where the little anxiety gremlins get to work and we feel various degrees of stress. The effect of stress is to increase our blood sugar level which is converted into glucose which is released into the blood, giving an energy boost. So far this sounds fine but then another result of this process is that insulin is automatically released as well, and insulin produces side effects of sweat and makes us dry-mouthed. So, we have a Catch-22 situation where, if we want the buzz before we speak, we end up with the dry mouth and being sweaty, and dry-mouthed and sweaty detracts somewhat from enjoying the buzz of walking out to wow the audience. Actually, I think it bizarre that our mouths go dry, while at the same time, hands and armpits seem anything but lacking in moisture! Another effect of stress is to give us mind block – when we are stressed, we use all available working memory and the result is that our minds go blank!

The trick is to use some simple techniques to slow the metabolic rate (have a normal heart beat and breathing pattern) and so trick the brain into thinking all is well (what audience?-

it's all a dream!).

Simple solutions for nerves

1 Develop a pre-talk routine

Peak performance athletes have a strict pre-race routine to help settle their nerves but keep them focused on the job in hand. These are both practical and psychological. For a speaker, the routine is different but the outcome is the same – total focus on the job in hand from start to finish. Kriss Akabusi has a saying which I think is really helpful – *'When you are in the arena, you need to be in the arena.'* When you have a practical routine to settle you down, then your focus is on the mechanics of giving the talk, which in turn distracts you from the feelings of anxiety you might be having. So what might be practical and psychological components of a speaker's pre-event routine?

● Check the room layout and, when you are confident everything is in place, take a deep breath and imagine the audience enthusiastically clapping at the end of your talk. See smiling faces in front of you and remember positive feedback you've had from other events.

● Eat sensibly. Whatever time you are speaking at, make sure you've had something easily digestible, satisfying and energy-giving an hour or so before you speak. If you are speaking directly after a dinner don't overdo anything fatty, acidic and in particular gassy, prior to standing up – it will stand up with you and introduce itself to the audience! The mistake is to not eat because you are nervous – that will result in an organ recital mid-way through your talk and the organ will be playing from deep within your digestive tract. Another point about avoiding eating because of nerves is that you will feel faint.

● Find a quiet spot to settle yourself just before you are due to speak – toilets are wonderful oases of calm! If you're the after-dinner speaker, you can settle yourself before the meal begins and do your breathing exercise before you stand up.

© AEOWENS 2005

● Adopt a short breathing exercise pattern before you go on the platform. If you are tense, it will make you short of breath and the danger of that is hyperventilating – another way to feel faint or dizzy (accompanied by sparkling lights in front of your eyes!). If you are short of breath, you will also end up rushing what you are saying to get it out before you run out of air. When you are standing in the wings and you're about to go up, take a deep breath and fill your lungs with oxygen, hold that for a moment and release it slowly. Repeat that twice more. As you breathe in the first time, imagine yourself putting all your tension in your lungs and as you breathe out release that tension. On the second time, breathe in peace and breathe that peace out into the room. On the third breath, breathe in confidence and breathe that confidence into the room – in a sense you are *creating the arena* you are about to step into, one of peace and confidence. When you come off the platform at the end, take a deep breath and relax.

To sum this section up – walk the track, prepare your mind, settle your body and relax your heart.

2 Keep it in perspective

I love the Charlie Brown cartoon in which Snoopy has been asked to look after Lucy's balloon. After a long day holding the string, he finally yawns and the balloon floats away. She is mad, but his reaction is, *'Two hundred years from now, who will care!'*

If you were to consider which was most important; your son's birthday, an anniversary, seeing your daughter's graduation or giving a great talk, which would rank highest? I don't mean that it's not fantastic to be rated highly as a speaker, but there are other things that will always be higher up our priority list. When you go to an event and are feeling nervous, think of something else on your priority list – it doesn't have to be family but could, for example, be a forthcoming business meeting that might lead to a major contract, a game of golf, a meal with great friends and so on. The effect of getting the talk in perspective means that you live by your priorities and will get maximum enjoyment from everything you do.

Another important part of keeping it in perspective is simply to remember that the people in the audience all have their own story to tell. You may see a sea of faces but it is guaranteed that among the audience will be those who've just had some bad news, are unwell, insecure, having problems with their neighbor, just come back from a great business trip or whatever. In short, they face all the ups and downs that you face – they are just people who need to know they are valuable.

3. Have an ace up your sleeve (not literally!)

You've had your intro, you are into the first three minutes which you've now got off by heart and are using this time to relax into the audience. You have your talk outline on cards ready to prompt should you need them. It's also really handy to have a few interesting and totally irrelevant facts, figures or quotes to hand. When your mind goes blank at any point during the talk, you can stay relaxed because you have something up your sleeve to use until you find your place. You may be a few feet away from the notes when you realize you've forgotten what you are meant to say next. You pause and almost as an aside throw out a funny statistic or quote as you make your way back to crib your notes, for example, _'Did you know that 35% of the population of the first world read their horoscopes?.'_ It will all seem part of your delivery style – interestingly these bizarre facts can often be one of the main things the audience remembers!

Cinderella meets Prince Charming

> _'It is like the comment Big Ben could make to the Leaning Tower of Pisa: 'I've got the time if you've got the inclination.'_
> Adlai Stevenson

The venue is checked, nerves are under control, you step onto the platform with an audience-centered mindset. You know the audience is (96%) happy to go with you and you're feeling relaxed and confident. One question you must have answered well before this is what to wear for the 'ball.'

Dressing for the Ball

For a man invited as after-dinner speaker, the answer is very straightforward – black tie and jacket unless the brief dictates otherwise. Other than that, for both genders, it is equally straightforward – wear what reflects you as a professional person. For some, that means smart and casual and for others a suit. I know that some briefs stipulate that the speaker should wear a business suit but so long as the speaker is professional in appearance, it doesn't have to be a suit.

We lived in Europe for a couple of years and one of the things I most admired was meeting top business people wearing smart, informal attire. It is worth having a session with an image consultant because we often wear colors that we love but that don't really suit us. One speaker always wore a black suit and black shirt because he just loved black and he felt great in them. He had a pale complexion and the effect of the black was to make him look ill. He took advice, kept the suit but changed the color of his shirt – the results were great. Whatever you wear, it is worth investing in really good clothes as they hold their cut and will last for ages.

A few pointers are:

- Invest in a few versatile and excellent quality clothes and shoes

- Wear colors that suit you but don't draw attention in the wrong way – bright yellow jackets against a green backdrop with a white screen just doesn't lend itself to relaxed audience eyeballs.

- Stick to styles that flatter – no matter what your body shape, there are ways of wearing clothes that will look good.

I also thought I'd take advantage of this section to get you to think about your general health. Here are a few questions:

- Do you look after your skin – do you have regular facials to keep your skin fresh and moist? I especially include you men here.

- Do you eat healthily, take regular exercise and watch your weight (high blood pressure is not helpful when added to platform stress!)

- Do you take regular time off just to relax

- How is your body odor – and do you keep your breath nice and fresh

Remember whatever happens:

> *'Years wrinkle the skin, but to give up enthusiasm wrinkles the soul.'*
>
> Sam Ullman

How to approach the prince

> *'Behold the turtle. He makes progress only when he sticks his neck out.'*
>
> James Conant

When Cinderella arrived at the palace, she was caught up in a process that would inevitably lead to her having to go into the ballroom. Passed from events organizer to introducer, she had to walk in to meet Prince Charming – did she do it as the poor girl from below stairs? Not on your life! She looked fantastic, she believed she was fantastic and it showed. When she was presented to him, she didn't look at the floor or the ceiling but straight into his eyes.

Speakers needs to remind themselves that the reason they are there is because they are the right person for that audience.

You've done all the preparation and so walk on the platform with confidence and purpose. Anticipate how much you will enjoy delivering your material. Everyone develops his or her own particular style of entrance – Geoff Burch, for example, does a very neat circuit of the stage on a small motorbike and he does so very elegantly and with great timing – so develop the style that conveys your sense of confidence and purpose.

- **Eye contact**: because standing in front of an audience makes us feel vulnerable (and nervous), it is easier to focus on the back wall, the ceiling, someone's tie or whatever, rather than members of the audience. The best way to walk the talk of confidence is to look the audience in the eye – even if it is a large auditorium and you can't see a thing! Keep your focus on what you are delivering to the audience so that someone not smiling back, or seemingly half asleep won't throw you. There will be some people in the audience who are positively responding to you as a speaker. Be encouraged by them and speak as if the whole audience was like them.

  One tall speaker was on a raised platform that caused her to have to lower her head to make eye contact and, on the video replay, it looked as if she was talking to the carpet!

  So watch out for that when you do your pre-talk check.

- **Open body language**: once you're positioned on the platform keep your body language open and use movements wisely. If you are going to emphasize a point with a particular gesture, don't overdo it. Also beware of unconscious body movements which suggest you are nervous or overconfident, for example, winking at the audience or fiddling with keys in your pocket. I remember watching a speaker both during his speaking session and the Q & A that followed. He had a habit of twiddling the fingers of his right hand against his right cheek every time he stopped talking. After a while the audience became riveted and increasingly tense as each pause was accompanied by the inevitable twiddle – I left before my nerves caved in! Make sure that you have a video taken of your performance every few months and analyze your verbal and non-verbal skills to make sure no bad habits have crept in.

- **Talk positively**: one of the pitfalls of insecurity is using self-deprecating humor. When Cinderella was introduced to the prince, she didn't start to protest that she was really a dowdy chambermaid whose only friends were singing mice! She didn't say she hoped she was worth the money the good fairies had spent on her ball gown or the Prince really should have chosen the professional dancing guru unfortunately already engaged at another ball.

Taking to the dance floor

Audiences almost never remember much of what a speaker says but they do remember how they *made them feel*. The Prince had a moment of real significance on the dance floor and the watching crowd didn't look at Cinderella's dancing technique – they were caught up in the happiness of the pair dancing.

One of the key things to think about when you're on the platform is how you can use *movement* to change the energy in the room. If you sense people are tired or have been sitting and listening for quite a while, coming onto the platform confidently and with energy will change the dynamics in the room. If, on the other hand, the speaker or program content before you has been a bit intense, then you can walk on confident, relaxed and using the pace of your words to help unwind the audience.

Be *flexible* to respond to the mood of the audience and if you sense it is necessary, ditch some material, move on to another section, or forget the PowerPoint, if it keeps the dynamics just right.

Taking to the platform is not a popularity contest – you're not responsible for the audience but you *are* responsible for the preparation leading up to walking on stage. What you put in is a direct correlation of what you and the audience will get out of the talk and this is revealed once you get on the platform. No matter how many times you've spoken or told the same story or joke, it has to sound as fresh as if it was the first time you told it. Every speaking event has to be approached as if it was your first ball.

You've prepared according to the brief, you've got the beginning, middle and endings all prepared, you've kept yourself focused and left nerves behind. All that you need to do is enjoy yourself. If you find yourself losing your focus, then go back to your cue cards where you have written at the top the couple of words you've used to keep you relaxed and on target. It is no different from watching a TV program when the phone rings – we can momentarily be distracted but can learn to tune back in very quickly (and ignore the phone!).

Whatever is going on around you as you talk – something falling over, a mobile phone going off, someone getting up to leave early – just focus on what you are doing and keep going. If there is a major problem, for example someone talking a bit loudly or people coming in late and taking their seats, you can either carry on or pause for a couple of seconds. Different speakers have different ways of reacting. Some speakers feel quite comfortable just carrying on with their talk, others prefer to pause and wait for stillness and still others would be tempted to draw attention to the person/s responsible! It is probably wisest not to engage in banter, unless it is a very small audience. The likelihood is that the banter would really embarrass the person on the receiving end and might antagonize others – who will then really look forward to putting you on the spot at the question and answer session.

Props and visual aids

This is a good time to mention props and visual aids. Depending on the subject of your talk and the level of audience participation the brief requires, props can be very useful. Visual tools can be very powerful and simple to use in illustrating a point. For example, talking about burnout and holding up an example of a never used epitaph – *'I wish I'd spend more time at the office'* – makes the point you're making pretty clear.

Diagrams on flipcharts are also really useful as well as inviting someone in the audience to write things down on the flipchart for you. It's important to use visual aids and props *strategically* rather than carry along a magician's suitcase full of fun options and then trying to use them all just because you brought them. I can't quite imagine how the story would have ended if Cinderella had taken to the dance floor carrying the cellar key, spare pumpkins, party hat, exploding crackers and a couple of spare mice – just in case!

The key to good visual aids is to use ones that require the *minimum of fuss* to set up, are least likely to go wrong and won't give the volunteer a heart attack. Remember there are such things as health and safety regulations, so whatever you are planning, make sure it won't end up with your requiring the services of a lawyer!

Question and answer sessions (which may include having to handle the ugly sisters)

In Chapter 2, I mentioned the lemon suckers and there will

always be one or two people who will not be predisposed to show a happy face and say pleasant words. I was recently at a masterclass where the speaker went down extremely well. The room was buzzing and I turned round to chat to an older business couple who were on their own. Smiling, I asked how they had enjoyed the evening, to which the reply came that it was a scandalous waste of money and on they went. They then proceeded to wait for the beautiful buffet and stayed on until the very last people left – still on their own and having talked negatively about the event to anyone they spoke to. I discovered afterwards that their mission in life seemed to be to attend events and minge (a lovely Scottish word for moan, pronounced like 'hinge').

So leaving the lemons behind what else can happen at Q & A sessions.

1 **No one wants to ask any questions** – if you're relaxed about it, so will your hosts and the audience. Usually when no one asks a question, you'll discover that the ones who would like to but didn't, will come and ask them after the event anyway. Sometimes the facilitator will ask a question which then leads on to other questions coming from the audience. It may also be that you've been so good with your content that there are genuinely no questions to be asked at that time. That's fine.

2 **You get a question that you don't know the answer to** – that's fine too. In general, if you've done all your preparation and are working within your field of expertise, you will be able to answer most questions. If it is a highly specialized field where there is always new material on the Internet, then you can quite easily and honestly say, for example: that's something you'd like to find the answer to yourself, or ask the person to see you afterwards so you can find the answer and get back to them with it at a later date. Another solution, depending on the audience and subject matter, is to ask if anyone in the audience has come across this particular question before and has an answer. The main

thing is, don't bluff your way through a question that deals with facts and figures or get engaged in a debate over something that will ruin the good effects of your platform session. Know your limits – *'The difference between genius and stupidity is that genius has its limits!.'*

3   **Someone makes a statement about your content** instead of asking a question, for example, *'I don't agree with what you said about letting staff go who are non-motivated'* or *'I found I dealt with this situation in a much better way,'* and so on. These can sometimes be useful comments that can be acknowledged and used to reinforce your message. Other times, they are from people who want to be noticed and so they make a statement that reflects their expertise in a way which comes across as patronizing. This is another reason why we need to have good self-esteem. When we are confident about who we are, we don't need to take offence at someone else's response to us.

4   **People will ask a question in order to incorporate a totally separate issue.** For example, you've spoken on marketing and a question is raised which seems legitimate but contains an internal red herring. For example, *'You mentioned letting people go who are not motivated but I can't afford to send my staff to a fitness gym every day. If I had my way everyone would go to the gym every day and eat organic food. Why doesn't the government give us more access to ...'* We've moved from motivation to stress to keeping fit to the hidden agenda: access to government funds! Don't get sucked into answering elements of a question that don't relate to the seminar subject.

> *'Never argue with a fool. Someone watching*
> *may not be able to tell the difference!'*
>
> Anon

5   **There are loads of questions and not enough time** – great. If you have a good facilitator, then let him handle the session, ensuring it stops when it should. If you have been

left to do that, make sure you notice who has raised their hands – it may mean you have to interrupt someone who has started to ask their question, in order to let someone who has been patiently and silently waiting, to ask theirs. If someone starts to monopolize the session with either a long-winded question, or they keep asking follow-on questions to each of your replies, you need to give an answer followed immediately by acknowledging someone else waiting with their question.

Catching the Midnight Coach – otherwise known as exiting the platform

This is the bit where Cinderella ruined an otherwise fantastic performance. She had come with a great introduction (fantastic pumpkin coach, coachmen and an outfit to die for), did a wonderful piece of work in engaging with the Prince and he had really bought in to her message and then what happens? She rushes off, leaving a glass slipper behind and is seen disappearing into the distance with some mice and a fast moving pumpkin! The audience was left confused and the Prince bemused – the only take-away he got from this encounter was a slightly worn shoe!

Whenever the session ends, whether it involves a question and answer session or not, make sure that when the applause ends, you leave as confidently and positively as you came onto the platform – no matter what happens. This goes back to what we looked at in chapter one about having confidence in who you are as a person and that your value is not tied into how you feel other people are responding to you.

Practical checklist -
for those going to the ball

1 Prepare a venue checklist (see Appendix 3)

2 Travel bag checklist (see Appendix 4)

3 Plan a pre-event routine to minimise nerves.

4 Book a health and fitness check-up if you haven't had one for the last six months

5 Look at your dress style and image - would it be a good idea to see an image consultant?

6 What techniques do you have to handle Q & A sessions?

5

The House that Frank Built

'The difference between 'commitment' and 'involvement' is like a ham and eggs breakfast – the chicken was 'involved,' the pig was 'committed."

Unknown

There is only one way to build your business as a speaker and it involves consistent commitment – in short, hard work. I'm going to cover this stage by stage, starting with the foundations on which everything rests – yes, you're right, we're back to good office infrastructure! Just like the Bible story of the wise man and the foolish man, if your office systems are well set up, then in the midst of lots of bookings, telesales, preparing web sites and so on, you will be less likely to make administrative errors like double-booking for two major clients!

The office

Whether you're working from a home-based office or use your work office, the components are exactly the same in terms of good practice. I really believe in letting others do the things we're not strong at so that we are free to do the things we do best. If you are not good at office work, then bring in someone who is so that your energy is focused on the right things – speaking and building your business.

In very practical terms what you need to have in place is:

- a **user-friendly filing system** (if you break a leg could someone go in and put their hands on the file you need?).

- a **very tight procedure system for processing enquiries** to either a firm offer of work or filed as 'dead': keeping hard copies of emails, notes on dates and content of phone conversations, penciling in diary dates etc. It is vital to keep written records of preliminary conversations with clients and bureaus. If a fee or add-on to the speaking session is discussed verbally but not confirmed on paper, it is not uncommon for both parties to have very differing recollections of what fee or timings were agreed in the first place. It can look like one party is trying to take advantage of the other. As with the train, let the check list take the strain!

- an **equally tight procedure system for issuing letters** of engagement, contracts, invoices etc.

- an **especially tight system for keeping financial records**: bills, invoices, receipts etc (especially for those vat registered!). If you're not methodical or comfortable about running accounts, then use a bookkeeper and a good accountant – believe me, in the long term it will save you money!

- a **comprehensive database** for enquiries, telesales, post-conference follow-up etc. This also means a good computer, fax and phone system

- a **high quality of stationery** – there is nothing that dispels a bureau or potential client's confidence in the speaker's ability than getting their promotional material on the equivalent of loo paper!

- a good supply of **coffee** or de-stressing herbal teas!

Before I started my business, I spent three months setting up the computer system, office infrastructure, bank account (my leap of faith!), stationery, contracts, web site and, most importantly, my planned strategy for growth. During those three months, I kept a very low profile so that I could concentrate on getting the foundations as right as possible, then, when I went public, I hit the road running. I didn't need to worry about what to do with a business enquiry as the procedure checklist was in place and, as the business evolved, I adapted and improved the original checklists.

The story is told of a couple of hunters who were flown deep into the wilds of Canada to hunt elk. They shot more than the helicopter could carry back but the hunters insisted that the previous year the other pilot of the same type of helicopter had managed to fly them out with all the elk they'd shot. Reluctantly, the pilot took off and a short time later they crashed. As they climbed out the wreckage, one hunter asked the other if he recognized where they were to which the reply came, 'I think we made it three miles past where we crashed last year.' Progress is progress no matter which way it comes about!

Marketing – or the story of the five little pigs

There's a little nursery game played using a child's toes which goes like this.

'This little piggy went to market (involves holding one toe)
This little piggy stayed at home (involves holding another toe)
This little piggy had roast beef (or a GM-free, organic veggie -burger!)
This little piggy had none (aaah!)
And this little piggy went 'weeheehee all the way home'
(involves tickling the foot).

Of the five pigs, only one went to the marketplace. Of the other four, one stayed at home and waited for the market to come to him and the others didn't seem to have grasped the seriousness of the situation at all!

The market never comes to us unless it recognizes that we have established a reputation and proven track record for success. So what do we need to go into the marketplace and be noticed among the many others perhaps saying the same thing?

The first thing is to recognize that the product you are selling is *yourself*, the second thing is to identify is how that product is *packaged*. We've already covered the qualities needed for a speaker, so let's look at the elements of the packaging.

1. 30-second pitch

You need to be able to say to someone in 30 seconds exactly what your business is all about. People will decide whether they want to hear more if those first 30 seconds have caught their interest, so be clear about what you want to say. A helpful tip is say it with a warm smile – even on the phone a smile communicates!

The obstacle many people face with the 30-second pitch is that they have the Mother Hubbard mentality – there are so many ideas and projects running about the place that could be used to describe what they do that they feel harassed. The solution is simple, find some of the 'kids' new homes and work with the ones that fit into your house! Mother Hubbard types usually have an HR or training background!

2. Biographies and promotional material

For a bureau, a great biography is a superb sales tool. It is not a bureau's job to develop and produce your material – it is such a joy for me when someone sends me a good video, DVD, audio-tape along with a clear statement of what they do and an accompanying biography that is not saturated with 'awesome, dynamic, phenomenal' and such like. If I have spare time, I don't mind editing and putting a biography together but I rarely have that time and, while I have scanners and publishing programs, I don't spend enough time on them to be quick at inserting photos. The other point is that a speaker has to have a biography that they feel reflects them so it is always better for them to produce it.

A biography should leave the reader with no questions – in short, they know who the speaker is, where he or she has come from, what is on offer and some sample clients, feedback comments – and a great photo! The key is 'less is more.' I get lots of biographies and the worst ones are where they have written their entire life history in font size 4 so that they can get everything onto the A4 page! Go to web sites and see what other speakers have done – you will notice that biographies will be revisited at least once within a year and upgraded to make it both reader and bureau friendly.

If you have good material that might be considered by a publisher as a book, then explore writing the book. If nothing else, the process of putting pen to paper will really clarify what you do, the kind of content you have and will provide additional material for yourself as a speaker. For smaller booklets, for example, tips on self-development or a pocket book of motivating thoughts, then you could consider self-publishing. This kind of material along with CDs and audio tapes are very handy for selling at venues where you speak or can be ordered by delegates. Many companies are very happy to buy a speaker's product as part of the delegate pack. Make sure your contact details are on all your products.

3. Web sites

Web sites are a great way of people seeing what you have to offer, products you have, client feedback, contact details and even video clips of you on the platform. You can advertise events where you will be speaking and the great thing about web sites is that it saves spending unnecessary money on lots of glossy brochures – which is fine when you're making lots of money. If you can do your own web site that is fine, remembering the word 'professional' – I have seen some sites that would be more at home in a Flintstones movie. If you use a web designer, make sure you've seen samples of their work or they come recommended. I was really fortunate when I first started, as someone recommended to me NB Media, a company with a journalist backgrounds. It meant that they gave superb suggestions about the initial web site and ran a development plan for my company web site. They monitor traffic, suggest improvements to the site, handle press releases, marketing the Tailored Talks Masterclass series and do a fantastic job. As with using a good secretary and bookkeeper, a good web site designer can take the monkey off your back leaving you free to get on with building your speaking business.

4. The Press

Raise your profile by writing articles for magazines and journals and get to know a couple of journalists who might do an interview for the local paper. Journalists are always looking for bits of information that can be used to fill in the columns on a quiet day. If you are running a new series of seminars, holding a one-day event, having a book published or working with local school kids, *let the press know*. You can also email clients with your own in-house newsletter with regular updates.

Setting up your stall

The product is packaged so now we need to take it to the marketplace.

There are two ways of setting up your stall and they can work in tandem. The first is to set out to build your own speaking business and the second is to make use of bureaus and agents.

1. Building your own business

'Courage is not the absence of fear, but rather the judgment that something else is more important than fear.'
Ambrose Redmoon

When you believe that what you can do will change people's lives, it gives you the confidence to overcome the trepidation you might feel when 'selling yourself' to build your speaking business. Remember that you are a *unique* and *significant* individual – there is no-one else that could replace you on the face of the earth. That in itself is a great reason for good self-esteem – use that self-belief to build your speaking business. In practical terms, there are some simple and necessary action steps that need to be taken to get your business built:

- **Telesales** – set time aside each day to systematically phone potential clients. Have a checklist of who has been phoned, what the result was and when they should be contacted again. Aim to contact different types of businesses – think laterally.

- Make the most of every event you speak at to gain a wider **network** of contacts, for example, get business cards, the delegate list, and ask for testimonials that can be used to build up your client portfolio. Make use of your promotional material that has all your contact details – everyone who has your contact details has their own expanding circles of contacts and you never know when they might pick up your leaflet and recommend you as a speaker to another company.

- Build good **working relationships** with events organizers – lunches are a great time to meet and chat. With the arrival of Costa, Starbucks and sushi places (not that I'm dropping any hints!), it is easy to make the effort to make yourself known to businesses and bureaus.

- Don't get discouraged if bookings get cancelled or an initial enquiry doesn't come to anything, that's just life .

- Use a specialist **speaker marketing consultant.** Someone like Philip Allen will spend time to strategically plan and help implement a speaker's development program.

- Work with an **established fee schedule** which reflects your take-away, and therefore, market value. We mentioned fee integrity in Chapter 2 and this is really important. Set a fee reflecting your value and increase that annually if you're feedback confirms that is appropriate. Have a favorite charity that will benefit from some of your bookings – there is a great Biblical proverb that says: *'One man gives freely and only grows richer, another withholds what he should give and only suffers want.'* Clients respect speakers who are involved in putting back into the community some of the financial benefits of their expertise.

● Make use of **professional speaker seminars** so that you are mixing with others who can help refer you to potential clients and vice versa. If another speaker is unable to take a booking for whatever reason, they will be happy to put forward someone else they know. While there are lots of speakers out there, there is also a huge marketplace. If you can go abroad for the experience of seeing how other speakers develop, that can be very useful both for developing your own style and for networking.

● Remember that **selling yourself** as a speaker does not mean you're losing your dignity, rather it reflects confidence in what you have to offer.

● Work with your **mentor** to keep stretching your skills. Your hard work will pay off even if it seems difficult at times.

A Guru was so impressed by the spiritual progress of his disciple that he left him to continue on his own at his little hut by a river. Each day the disciple would wash out his loin cloth – his only possession – to dry, and one day found it torn to shreds by rats. He had to beg for another from the villagers but when the rats nibbled this one too, he got himself a cat. The rats were gone but now he had to beg for milk for the cat along with his own food. This was too much trouble so he got a cow. But he had to beg for fodder and decided it would be easier to till the land around his hut but that left no time for meditation, so he employed laborers to till the land. This was more work, so he married a wife to share the task with him and before long he was one of the wealthiest men in the village.

Years later, the Guru happened to drop by and was surprised to see a palatial mansion where the hut once stood. He asked a passerby if this wasn't the place where his disciple used to live. Before he got his reply the disciple came out of the mansion. 'What's the meaning of this my son?' To which the man replied, 'You're not going to believe this, but it was the only way I could keep my loincloth!'

2. Bureaus and agents

The one thing bureaus are not short of is speakers! Every bureau will get letters, promotional material and emails from people wanting to put themselves forward to be used for events. There are a few things that really help in the working relationship with a bureau.

- Be *professional* in your approach – work to the brief and maintain high standards of delivery.

- Keep them *up-to-date* with what you are doing – recent speaking events or personal achievements, e.g. driving at 200 mph in a brand new Lotus racing car around the Malaysian Grand Prix circuit (this may not sound amazing but if I told you Miles Hilton Barber, who is blind, was at the wheel at the time, it makes for riveting reading!).

- Give them up-to-date *promotional material.*

- Be *easy to reach* and return phone calls quickly. There are other speakers who will be being approached as well as you and often the first available one who can commit to the date will get the booking.

- *Invite* them to come and hear you if that is practical.

- If you get bookings that lead to further work, *remember the commission* due to the bureau/agent. When a speaker sends a check a year or two after an event because it resulted in more work down the line, the bureau will always be very appreciative at the integrity shown – and guess who they will be keen to continue to promote!

There can be a few downsides to working with some bureaus and I mentioned one or two of these earlier in the book.

- The fee the end client is charged can sometimes involve commission from more than one bureau so while the speaker gets his fee, the client may have paid substantially more than that. The speaker's reputation can suffer and it can be galling to realize that the money being paid for your session is mostly going elsewhere.

- The brief may not have been properly researched.

- A speaker, with a name or reputation, may be put forward to speak at an event which is inappropriate for their skills.

- A speaker may end up being phoned by several different bureaus all trying to get the work from the same client. In some instances they may suggest that the speaker lowers his fee for a variety of reasons so that they can secure the booking. This doesn't necessarily mean that the client is being charged less.

As with all good things in life, the best shine through and you'll be able to find the bureaus that have the integrity and professionalism you are looking for.

Frank's Useful Checklist

1 What areas of your office infrastructure need consolidating?

- Equipment: phone, fax, computer, mobile, files
- Procedures for enquiries and firm bookings
- Bookkeeping
- Stationery
- Staffing - bookkeeping, secretarial etc

2 What areas of your marketing strategy need developing or refreshing?

- 30 second pitch
- Biography
- Promotional material
- Networking
- Marketing plan
- Telesales
- Web site
- Professional development seminars
- Relationship with clients and bureaus

6

Wise Words from the Masters

I mentioned a couple of times the great benefits that can come from having a mentor – someone who journeys alongside you for a season as you continue on the journey of excellence. In this chapter, I'm handing over to some of the best so that you can hear their words of wisdom. Whatever stage we are at as speakers, knowing how to excel always takes us back to basics, so without further ado let's hear from some of the best.

Allan Pease, speaker and co-author, with his wife Barbara, of best selling books 'Why Men Lie and Women Cry' and 'Why Men Don't Listen and Women Can't Read Maps.'

First impressions count and research shows that people form the majority of their opinion of someone within the first 90 seconds of meeting them.

This knowledge is useful in day-to-day life, but acting on it is especially important as a speaker where you need to look confident, capable and self-assured. As you walk on the platform, the audience's opinion will be predominantly based on non-verbal communication – this includes facial expressions, eye contact, tone of voice, body posture and motions, clothes and the way that you use silence.

Making the right entrance is the first step to your success. Humans, like other animals, are territorial and likely to perceive the platform as hostile territory, which makes you decrease your speed as you enter a new space. However doing this can make you look as though you lack confidence, so you need to make a point of going on to the platform at an even speed.

Even if your stomach is churning with nerves, you can mask this simply by smiling. Inexperienced speakers can get the confident walk right while at the same time looking tense. A genuine smile shows confidence and can make you warm to an audience before they have even said a word.

Keep your body language open and avoid any 'barrier postures,' such as folding your arms, as it could give the message that you are nervous, negative or defensive, even if you are not.

Once you have made it past the introduction to your talk, initial impressions have been made, but remember that your body language during the rest of your session can further influence the audience.

Keeping eye contact conveys candor and openness and elicits a feeling of trust. Obviously, staring too intently into their eyes will make them think you are a crazed idiot, so you need to get that right. Once you're in full flow, you should try to subtly mirror your audience's movement and posture. If you can do this and still maintain eye contact while still appearing natural, the audience will concentrate on you and not on what you're doing.

Using your body language in the right way will convey the message of a well-balanced and confident individual. Now all you have to do is worry about getting the content right.

L **Thank you, Allan, and now over to another globe-trotting speaker, <u>Miles Hilton-Barber</u>. I met Miles over a year ago and was bowled over by his achievements and his delightful personality. He is blind and has used that to challenge himself to do amazing things – with an exceptionally witty sense of humor.**

'You never get a second chance to make a first impression!

Whether you are visiting a potential agent, or walking onto a speaker platform, dress for the position/status you are aiming at, not how others may perceive you now.

'We judge ourselves by what we feel capable of doing, while others judge us by what we have already done.'
Henry Wadsworth Longfellow (1807-1882)

Hearts communicate with hearts, and heads communicate with heads. Beware of preparing a slick, flawless presentation that lacks passion. The world is full of speakers with fantastic, flawless PowerPoint presentations and immaculate, glossy handouts that cannot be either faulted or remembered. Passion speaks volumes more than perfection. Be remembered! If you lack passion and personal conviction about your subject, your chances of leaving a lasting impression are slim indeed.

If you are as nervous as a long-tailed cat in a room full of rocking chairs, here is a tip that will help! Focus on the needs of the audience, and how you are planning to meet them through your presentation – not your own nerves! You are seeking to sow seeds in their heart, to improve the quality of their lives. If you go out there burdened for the needs of the people, you will more likely succeed than if you go out worrying about what sort of impression you will make. ALWAYS keep focused on the needs of the audience and what you can give them, not the reverse. If you can go onto the platform feeling totally confident and self-assured *with no nerves* ... BEWARE – you are losing your edge, and in danger of going downhill with your speaking.

Never take any audience for granted, no matter how small, how young, how old – treat them all with great respect, and throw all your focused energy and passion into it. Why? Because they deserve it, and, secondly, you never know who those people know, and what great invitations/contacts may result. Value and respect your audience, and they will value and respect you in return.

If you are nervous addressing a large audience, remember

that it only consists of a lot of individual people, who just happen to be sitting next to each other. There is no such thing as 'a crowd' in my mind – I speak to individuals.

In many ways, there is nothing new under the sun but I get to share my experiences which may help someone else. To put it another way, I am just a beggar, telling another beggar where to get a square meal!

In terms of constructive feedback, I always carry a small tape recorder with me onto the podium, and record my presentation.

It is often a very sobering experience to play it back afterwards. It never lies, it gives you the neutral facts about your presentation, and enables you to get much better – and more humble along the way! By the way, eating humble pie may stick in your throat at times, but it is healthy food indeed!

Always know exactly how you are going to start and finish your presentation – start brilliantly, finish brilliantly, and be great in-between!

Two old grannies watched a speaker go onto the platform, carrying a huge wad of notes. One observed to the other; 'If he can't even remember what he wants to say to us, how does he expect us to remember!'

Before you speak, and while you are speaking, you need to be crystal clear about the main points you are seeking to communicate. If you aren't sure yourself, be sure they won't be either!

Statistically, I understand only about 20% of our audience will remember and act on points from a motivational presentation. There is no room for complacency in our delivery, if our goal is to impact people's lives!

As a motivational speaker, I am always on the lookout for appropriate quotes and there are some great web sites around like **www.positivepress.com**. Likewise, humor is one of the most powerful communication tools and **Ajokeaday.com** specialize in good quality jokes for speakers. Whatever point you are seeking to make, look for a joke to illustrate that point

– but try to avoid telling jokes with no relevance or application to your talk or audience.

Motivational speaking after dinner – this is not an easy mix, especially if you do not know your audience. If in doubt, avoid it! I have sometimes found it quite successful, especially with a professional group wanting more than a senseless binge and a laugh after dinner.

Here is a quote that I think all speakers should memorize and contemplate on before they speak;

'I think the purpose of life is to be useful, to be responsible, to be honorable, to be compassionate. It is, after all, to matter, to count, to stand for something, to have made some difference that you lived at all.'

Leo C. Rosten

Finally, here are a couple of my favorite quotes:

'Being defeated is often only a temporary condition. Giving up is what makes it permanent.'

Marilyn vos Savant 1946

'Never be afraid to try something new. Remember, amateurs built the ark. Professionals built the Titanic.'

 When I asked <u>Nigel Risner</u> for his words of wisdom he said that greatest pearls of wisdom can be held in a child's hand – he likes to be succinct!

'As a speaker I always want to make sure that what I say and share is

    1 – **A**ccurate
    2 – **S**upportive
    3 – **K**ind

So to all you speakers, ASK your self *before* you start, will it cover all three. If not – don't speak.

It is an honor and privilege to stand before an audience, make sure you remember that.

L **And now for the wonderful <u>Maire Mosely</u>, a business psychologist with a great sense of humor.**

'I think my greatest advice to anyone thinking about speaking professionally for a living is to be truly *audience focused*. I come across people all the time who focus on their own needs rather than those of the audience.

Try to put yourself in the minds of the audience. How are they feeling? Do they want to be there or have they been sent a three-line whip telling them to attend? What's been happening in the organization? What are the issues or successes ? Are they feeling motivated? Is morale high or low? Why?

If you start to speak to an audience from where *they* are, you can then lift them to where you want to take them.

A different example …

Just recently, I wanted to send a PowerPoint presentation to someone for an event and I was told, 'We're not using PowerPoint. We need overhead transparencies.' I do know that, at the time of writing, PowerPoint projectors can be rather expensive to hire and, being conscious of budgets, I'm aware that some people can't stretch to the cost of hiring this equipment.

When I looked into it further, it transpired that one of the other presenters on the day found PowerPoint 'too fiddly' and didn't want to use it. It was then decided that everyone should use overheads instead of PowerPoint even though the room was fitted with all sorts of wonderful equipment that came at very little extra cost on the day rate.

In this day and age, overheads look unprofessional and old-fashioned. The audience expect you to use the most up-to-date equipment. That's what they're using at work and they expect you to be at least as up-to-date as them.

Marketing is something I can't stress this enough. Make time for marketing. The pattern of your bookings will change, however, the need for marketing will never change. If you don't make the time, people forget who you are. If they've forgotten you, they won't book you.

Jim Rhode, past President of the National Speakers Association gave me this advice early on in my speaking career and I never forgot it. It's been the best piece of advice I ever got. He said 'Marie, it's as simple as this – out of sight, out of mind. You must let people know you're there. Send them a Newsletter or a White Paper six to eight times a year.' By taking Jim's advice, I stay in contact with my clients and it has paid off not only in terms of building and maintaining relationships but also in terms of bookings. Make time for marketing. It needs to be a top priority.

 That is really useful advice and something Michael Jackson is really good at doing. Michael ran the highest Internet business in the world while climbing K2 and, for three days, carried to safety a sherpa with a collapsed lung. He runs the biggest Internet outdoor clothing business in Europe. His recently published book, 'Life's Lessons from History's Heroes' is rapidly becoming a bestseller.

When you stand up to speak, don't try to sound important or profound. Just imagine you are speaking to a room full of your best friends and trust that the words will come – preparation is congruent with trusting. So, when you stand up, you won't clam up.

Earlier in the book, I mentioned Robbie Glen, whose advice is written from the specific perspective of an after-dinner speaker.

In speaking, there is no substitute for preparation. Some 7 to 10 days before going to speak, I telephone the organizers to get a brief on the event and on what is expected of myself. I do this even in cases where I have been sent a brief as this often comes through third parties. I want to double check the venue, date, time and dress. Once when seeking details, I asked the organizer whether a function was formal and she replied that it was informal. I duly turned up in my lounge suit when it was a black tie affair. When the organizer and I compared notes, we realized how this misunderstanding had arisen and we managed to extricate ourselves by saying my suit carrier had been lost by the airline. It sounded plausible.

It is also essential to find out something of the organization which is hosting the dinner and what it expects of you to ensure everyone is on the same wavelength. It is also helpful to find out the make-up of the audience.

I also specifically ask the organizer how long he would wish me to speak. It is interesting that the most frequent reply which I receive is 'What do you think?' I always suggest that the optimum length of an after dinner speech is 25/30 minutes, this being dictated by bladder capacity rather than intellectual capacity. I am always astounded how many speakers disregard the wishes of the organizers and overstay their welcome at the lectern.

It is also helpful to learn of any other speakers and the order of speaking.

In preparing a speech, I visit my database of speeches. (Every speech I have given over the past 10 years I have on disc.) I look for the speech which most replicates what is being sought on this occasion and use this as a basis for my preparation. I also go through my computerized database of material and extract the material which I intend to use. This latter database has been assembled over many years from personal experience, from articles I have read or heard which have given me the inspiration to write. There is nothing better than personal experience to drive home a point or raise a laugh, as it has the ring of truth about it.

Digressing, before I put an article into my database of material, I write it out and then read it aloud. By reading it out, I find if my sentences are too long or if the words sound right together. Too many alliterations are to be avoided. I then transcribe it from the spoken word into the written before entering it in my database. I also annotate each item in my database with a source and date.

In compiling a speech, I always aim to include 50% more material than is required and will reduce the speech on delivery in accordance with responses I receive and what has gone before. I never introduce more than 10% new material to any speech. You can never be sure how material is going to be received and so you should introduce it gradually.

There are different ways to use notes for a speech. Indeed, some speakers do not use notes; some use bullet points, and others use verbatim notes. I use verbatim notes with the lines 1.5 spaced. It is what I feel comfortable with as I feel better able to deal with unexpected interruptions, e.g. a dropped plate or glass. I am immediately able to look down to see where I am. I find notes handy should it be that I wish to move from paragraph 1 to paragraph 3, while omitting paragraph 2. It would be easy to jump from paragraph 1 to paragraph 4, and, if you have a flow in your speech, you could never get back to paragraph 3. Although I have verbatim notes, I never read. I only use them for reference and guidance.

Sadly, because of the aging process and my reliance on bifocal glasses, I need to use a lectern. When traveling by car, I take one but this is not always possible when using other modes of transport.

When I arrive at a venue, I always go to the function suite to test the sound system. It is essential you are aware of the strengths of the system; how far you can stand from the microphone with your voice still being picked up and if the system picks up your voice when you move your head. You can listen to your voice coming back to make sure you can be heard. The other detail which I wish to know is where the organizer wishes me to speak from. The best position is that which gives you maximum eye contact.

I am always conscious of how much alcohol I consume before speaking. I have seen too many inexperienced speakers under-perform as a result of over indulgence. Some believe alcohol steadies your nerves. Experience has taught me that alcohol desensitizes one's antennae, making one oblivious to what is going on and unable to pick up the vibes from the audience.

Everyone who speaks in public has adrenaline flowing and this causes delivery to be faster than normal. For a number of reasons, this can present difficulties. The public address system speakers emit the sound at slightly differing times. Thus, if speech is too quick, the words can run together and become indistinguishable. If someone has an accent (it is never you who has an accent), speech which is slow and carefully pronounced is more likely to be followed.

Research shows 7% of the meaning of any conversation is contained in the words alone; the rest is communicated in body talk, a combination of posture, gesture, gaze and expression.

L **I was fortunate to get hold of Professor Peter McKiernan in a bistro in St. Andrews as he is usually run off his feet preparing new research at the University and gallivanting all over the world. So we went for the interview technique for his advice.**

Libby: Peter, you have gained a large reputation over many years on the speaking scene. Can you help me to draw out advice for new speakers on the circuit?

PMK;   I'd be delighted, but there is so much to learn. It is hard to know where to begin.

Libby: When did you first start public speaking?

PMK: It was nearly 25 years ago and I remember it like it was yesterday. It was a daunting experience. A talk to a bunch of Rotary Club folk – after dinner.

Libby: So you were nervous?

PMK: Very much so. But, as I worked on that speech, I got the best piece of advice I have ever had about overcoming nerves before an event. A wily old colleague, rich in life's experiences, witnessed my plight. He said, 'Before you go on, think of something completely unrelated to your speech that you know well and like very much. Then visualize it and memorize it, then recall it in the minutes before you get up to talk.' At the time, I played a lot of cricket and so I took the results of the latest test match against the West Indies and memorized the batting orders and the scores of the batsmen. As I sat through dinner that night, I struggled hard to recall them all, and after a lot of effort, I managed to get them all. By the time I rose to speak, I had no nerves at all. All my mental attention and adrenalin had gone into recalling the batting lists! The speech was not one of my best, but at least it did not put me off. I had mastered a technique to stop the nerves and that was worth it in itself.

Libby: Do you still get nervous?

PMK: Of course I do. I do not think that someone without nerves can take either the topic or the audience seriously. Even after 25 years and with speeches I know off by heart, I still get those rumblings and I still recall the same batting lists I learned all those years ago. It still works and I hope it never lets me down.

Libby: You mention the audience – that is very important for you, I know. Having listened to you talk several times, I am impressed with the attention to detail you take.

PMK: You're right, I may appear obsessive but I believe the audience is critical. I need to know their ages, their occupations, the gender and race breakdown, their aspirations for the event, their experiences with the topic, their number, their seating layout and so on. It affects everything that I do to prepare for them. They are my demand side and I have to supply something that suits their needs, wants and even desires. To do this, I need detailed information. And it doesn't stop there. I need to know who the other speakers are (if any) what their brief is, their topic and so on, so I can dovetail my material. I also insist on knowing the type of event – is it a motivational seminar, a recovery situation, a new product launch, a mind-changing experience. This governs how I will deliver the various elements of my speech.

Libby: When I have worked with you, you say there are two types of audience.

PMK: That's right, there is the client and there is the audience itself. The client's need and wants may equate to those of the audience. If this is the case, then all is well. But, it rarely comes down to this. The client wants something and assumes that the audience wants or needs the same thing. This is not always the case. So you end up with two sets of needs and wants and this makes it difficult to prepare any one speech that will deliver both sets of goods. The evaluation forms from the audience may be great but the client is not happy or vice versa! Hence, it is crucial to try and get agreement beforehand on the issues you have to address. This often means speaking with the reps of both groups. Often, this is tough as the client tends to dominate up-front talks. But in these talks, it is crucial to try and get across the notion of a different set of audience needs and what these may be. If you don't do this research, the speech will miss the mark. When French chefs are asked how they could ever prepare such wonderful meals in less than half an hour, they reply immediately-'it is all in the prep.' No prep, no success.

Libby: Given a choice, whose needs and wants come first?

PMK: Well, you have put me on the line here. In such a situation, I would always go with the client for two reasons. First, I make an assumption that they have an idea what the audience needs and second, they are paying the bill!

Libby: So, you mention a good trick to cope with nerves and a lot of sound research on the client and the audience before you start to prepare a speech. So what comes next?

PMK: Next is my preparation and presentation. What I gather from all the research informs the way I put the speech together, its content and its presentation. I focus on those things that will satisfy their needs well, even if this means throwing out a whole bunch of material that I think is excellent. You always have knowledge of this material as back up, so it is never a complete waste. Then prepare in threes: Intro, Main Content, Outro. Even my main content section will contain three telling points that I feel they need. This makes it easier to remember and also plays a good learning game as folk take things in better in threes. Any less and you have short changed them and any more and they will not remember it.

Libby: And on the day itself?

PMK: Again, lots of prep. By this time, you should know your content inside out – the way an actor know his lines. So move on and get the fundamental check sorted out. Arrive early, go straight to the room, check out lighting, sound, presentation equipment, acoustics etc. Don't be afraid to change things either. Often rooms are set up by casual labor who have no idea who is speaking and to whom. So move chairs or tables. I once moved a whole stage because the afternoon sun would have burned out all my graphics if it had stayed in its original position. This was much to the annoyance of the caretaking staff, especially as the sun did not shine that afternoon. But, as we say, we did prepare for it.

Libby: Anything here the most important?

PMK: Yes, make sure you know where the technician is now and throughout your talk. What can go wrong will go wrong and he or she will be critical in rectifying things. If and when it goes wrong, stay cool, make a joke about it (e.g. working with children, animals and technology ...) and have the technician right in your line of sight!

Libby: Any final nuggets of advice for new speakers?

PMK: Yes, your speech is going to fail sometime – even if you have read and digested this book from cover to cover. Contexts change overnight and on one gig, during my talk, a text message came through to one of the audience saying the company had sacked 50% of its work force. They did not know whether they were in the 50% or not. The whole room erupted, folk left to make urgent calls, others fretted miserably in corners and the few who remained were not focused at all. in other cases, I have failed because I simply misread the brief and did not do enough prep. You have to realize that none of these events makes you a bad speaker. The founder of the Honda motor company, Soichiro Honda, said, '99% of what I know comes from my failures and only 1% from my successes.' So, learn to fail. Do not let it put you off. You get better by breaking down the reasons for your failure and piecing it all back together again. And from your successes, learn not to be arrogant or conceited if it all goes well. Give yourself a pat on the back but recognize that a lot of other folk helped it happen, too.

Libby: Peter, many thanks for sharing these thoughts

with us today.'

Peter is a master of preparation. I remember for one brief, which I thought was really thorough, he came back and asked for the color of their socks – joking of course!

 Dave Thomas is the world's memory champion and is just great at keeping me up-to-date with material that I can use with clients.

Perception and reality – never the twain shall meet

As a speaker, I am always looking to improve my skills and I think that the best way to do it is to find great speakers and ask them how they do it. Why? Because in ten minutes they will tell you something it took them ten years to learn. So I found a fantastic speaker who lives near me in the Northern wasteland that is Yorkshire and every month for the past 4 years I have phoned him and asked him for his advice. One day after a long conversation, I asked him what his gem was for the day and he said that what I had to do was develop an aura. I asked him to explain a little further. He said that my impact as a speaker was all about the way that I dressed, walked, talked and held myself. He said I should develop it to the point where, when I walk into a room, the delegates automatically know that I am the speaker. I thought this was something definitely worth working towards. So I duly went out and bought myself a nice pair of shoes, shirt, tie and a tailor-made suit. In addition to this, I practiced my 'aura' every night in the mirror at home!

Shortly after I had been given this wonderful piece of advice that was going to propel my career to the stars, I was speaking at the Sheffield Hilton. Following me on to the platform was Roger Black, the Olympic silver medalist. I thought this would be a great chance to try out my new aura. I was due on the platform at 3pm so waited outside the conference room composing myself. I mused over what my friend had said and felt I knew exactly what he meant. After all, here I was, stood in the foyer of the Sheffield Hilton, with a business conference waiting to hear me speak. Roger Black, the Olympic silver medalist, was waiting to follow me on to the platform. I had my new suit, shoes, shirt and tie and I had my new aura. I had my name badge on saying David Thomas – Professional Business Speaker. I had arrived and this was a seminal moment in my speaking career. But just at that moment a guy walked through the door and said 'Is it alright if I park my car outside?'

Perception and reality – never the twain shall meet! Being a speaker is about being on a platform – but only a speaking platform. You have to connect with your audience with your astonishing expertise and experience. But you have to be prepared to show some humility as well. There will always be something or somebody out there who will bring you back down to earth with a bump if you get too big for your boots, whether they mean to do it or not.

 And now for advice from a different type of speaker, the stand-up comic. Ladies and gentlemen, Dave Wolfe.

The easy way to become an hysterically funny speaker

There isn't one.

I've been a comic for 29 years, starting via the then traditional route of holiday camps, working men's clubs, nightclubs, theatre, TV, radio. For the last thirteen years, I've concentrated solely on the corporate market, so after dinner speaking is now 'my thing'!

If you are just starting out, you won't want to hear this, but experience is my No.1 tip!

1) Experience

Take every opportunity to speak – practice makes perfect – don't turn it down because it might be tricky – you have to be bad before you improve, it's part of the learning curve.

If you don't like or agree with that last sentence, then stop reading now. Public Speaking is not for you. There is not one speaker or comedian who has never had a bad night. You learn more from your bad nights than you do from your good ones.

Volunteer to speak everywhere – golf clubs, weddings, private functions, 'Open Mic' spots at comedy clubs and so on.

Start by serving as master of ceremonies – there is very little pressure in hosting an event as you're not expecting the audience to hang on to your every word, and the practice is invaluable.

Confidence is extremely important, but real confidence is born through experience.

2) Preparation

As an MC, it is quite acceptable, in fact it's the norm, to have cue cards. Every event is different, so the MC needs these tools to ensure that the running order is adhered to. You will only be required to speak in short bursts, so try to learn the content of your next announcement and do it without the card; this will prepare you for speaking in your own right without the need for these memory aids.

When you graduate to presenting your own speech, never read a speech using a lectern – I've never seen it work convincingly – cue cards only, if you must!

Part of your preparation should always be to arrive early. Not only do you need to be fully briefed, but also you need to check out the sound system to make sure that it is set up properly. Arrange to meet the venue manager or sound technician an hour before the audience is due to arrive. Which brings me on to …

3) Microphone Technique

Ask a professional or a soundman how to use the mike

properly! I speak at hundreds of dinners, and so many amateur speakers blow their chances of a good reception because of their poor technique. If the audience can't hear you, you've no chance!

As a rule of thumb, speak directly into the mike – not across it. It should be approximately 4 inches from your mouth – and don't wave it around! If you move your head, the mike goes with you – OK!

4) Building your material

As an MC, your content will depend on the function and consist mainly of announcements and 'housekeeping.' As you gain more experience, you will be able to slip in the odd gag or anecdote.

This is fabulous experience as you will learn what works and what doesn't without too much pressure. (If a one-liner 'dies' it's not the end of the world as you are only seen as the link-man anyway!) By trial and error, you are now on the way to compiling material for your own speech.

5) Content

Many professional speakers make a fundamental error in judging their audience. They have a rule of thumb whereby if the audience is all male, then they can use profanities. The best corporate speakers never swear. It's seen as the easy option. Don't risk alienating your audience.

(There are notable exceptions, but I assume that if you are reading this you are not up to Billy Connolly's standard just yet! – besides Billy has his own audience, you don't! And Billy would never be so sexist as to swear solely in the presence of men!)

I often speak at Sportsmen's Dinners, and I never have a problem following a sporting celebrity who has used curse words. Quite the reverse, the audience usually appreciate the fact that I haven't insulted their intelligence.

6) Duration

As far as this is concerned, the old maxim holds true: Leave them wanting more!

A great five-minute speech is always better than a good twenty-minute one. Build it gradually, don't pad it. Don't use a gag unless you believe in it 100%.

If you're not convinced it's funny, you can't expect to convince an audience.

Most professional speakers are booked to do about 35 minutes. I feel more comfortable doing 45 to 50 minutes (although my 'personal best' was 2 hours, 20 minutes to a particularly entertainment-starved group of ex-pats in the Middle East!)

6) Delivery
Enjoy it!

By now you've gained experience and confidence as an MC, you've compiled gags and stories which hopefully are becoming 'routines,' now you're ready to speak! – So SMILE!

'Warmth' is the single most important element in a comic's armory.

Tommy Cooper or Ben Elton?

Les Dawson or Mark Lamarr?

If the audience like you, they will forgive you anything – your material, your delivery, your grubby suit! – anything.

Having said that, if you've got good material, delivery and a nice suit – add warmth and you're laughing.

And so are they.

 Talking tips from the Alternative Business Guru, Geoff Burch!

I had never seen a professional speaker, or ever been told what I could or couldn't do. So, when I did it and security carried me struggling from the venue, I used to hear them say to each other, 'Well, at least he's different!'

Moral – develop your own unique style, but don't be afraid to bend the rules.

Then, put yourself about everywhere – even if you have to work for nothing in those first critical months. Be seen again and again and again – unless you are crap and then you should hide under a rock until you are not!

Don't take on jobs you know in your heart you shouldn't be doing. However good the money is or however silver tongued the ego-massaging agent has been, when you are faced with a room full of drunken photocopier salesmen and their giggling, wiggling concubines, as the air turns green with flying sprouts, you will know this is one you should have turned down!'

L **The next and final wise words come from rumbling feelings within a. n. agent – who is respected on every continent in the world for integrity and professionalism.**

I heard somewhere that the average CEOs have over a hundred business books in their office but claim to have never read any – are business books that boring? Possibly!

So if the majority of business books are bought but never read, why do people buy them? More importantly, why do companies then hire the authors to speak at their conferences?

I used to say to prospective speakers the easiest way and best-known method to break into the speaking circuit was to write a book – but now I'm not too sure ...

I asked various people who have been providing speakers for some time how many top-class speakers are there in the UK? And you may be somewhat surprised that their response varied between being able to count them on one or two hands.

So why is there a distinct lack of top-class talent?

The answer lies in the fact that there are very few natural-born communicators who have an innate gift with words and those that do are invariably immersed in areas outside of the business world.

Perhaps that could explain why companies ask politicians to speak, although it seems incredible that organizations would want to mirror the achievements of pace, integrity and excellence aspired to in governmental departments.

Great speakers need to be entertaining – by making people laugh, you quickly disarm them (George W. please take note), and by using amusing anecdotes and hilarious experiences, people seem to relate to and remember the presentation for far longer.

Top-class speakers give off a feel-good factor that glows through an audience. Their warmth and integrity connect with people to sow the seeds for future development and fulfill their aspirations ... they act as a wakeup call to the slumbering potential within all of us.

Once our imagination is unleashed, it give us the incentive to take action and explore who we are, our values and what we want to become and go on to achieve. The effect is transformational as it involves our emotions that, once aroused, then act as a guide to stir us into action.

So, it's simple ... to be a top-class speaker you need have the story-telling ability of a politician, the wit of a comedian, the honesty and warmth of a priest, the eye of a painter, the imagination of an actor, and the confidence of a top class sports star.

Thank you, wise men and women!

What a timely reminder that we need to continually seek to develop what we do and how we do it, both for our own and our audience's benefit. And how liberating it is to discover that there is no one stereotype for success.

You've now had words of wisdom from both speakers and an agent, and here is a final word from Albert Einstein.

'I am enough of an artist to draw freely upon my imagination. Imagination is more important than knowledge. Knowledge is limited. Imagination encircles the world.'

7

Calling the Little Jedi

I thought it would be really helpful to write something specifically designed to meet the needs of teachers and pupils. The lack of confidence many adults have is a result of experiences which took place in their formative years. In Chapter 1, we looked at the triangle of insight, where how we react as an adult can often be determined by *patterns of response* adopted as a child. Schools in particular can either be a great nurturing ground or an endurance test depending on who else is in the class, the nature of the teacher and what is going on at home.

The effects of hard experiences for children are reflected in the statistics which show that in Scotland, for example, *one in four* Scottish children will suffer from depression before they reach adulthood. A World Health Organization survey revealed that Scottish 15- to 16-year olds felt less confident than their peers in 25 other countries. These figures reflect something which is happening throughout the whole of the UK, but the encouraging thing is these statistics *can be changed.*

In today's business environment, major changes are taking place and some forward-thinking companies are investing in creating a *permission-giving* culture for their staff. These companies recognize that internal change in an employee will contribute to a change of attitude towards the company and other colleagues. This brings a new dynamic to the business which creates a positive growth culture – the staff are proud of themselves, their product and the business cannot do anything but grow. Fear is replaced by courage.

On the other hand there are others who give the impression that it is not acceptable to be seen to be too successful – their cup is half empty rather than half full. This negative approach inhibits staff from realizing their full potential both on a personal and corporate level. Innovative thinking, permission giving and confidence need to cascade down, to be modeled from the top. When Gutzon Borglum was sculpting the head of Abraham Lincoln, the lady cleaning the studio stopped and asked, 'How did you know Abe Lincoln was inside that piece of stone?' The privilege and priority of those responsible for staff is to see what is there and facilitate its release – the challenge is to start with oneself!

In the beginning

In their early years, kids have great dreams which are a reflection of their openness to life and their expectation that great achievements can be theirs.

> *You may be familiar with the story of the little boy playing baseball in his backyard. He was talking to himself saying: 'I'm the greatest hitter in the world.' He then threw the ball in the air, took a swing at it and missed. 'Strike one!' He picked up the ball, tossed it higher in the air shouting 'I'm the greatest hitter in the world,' swiped at the ball, missed and cried 'Strike two!' With great determination he really lobbed the ball as high as he could, took an almighty swing and missed. 'Strike three – fantastic, I'm the best pitcher in the world!'*

Show and tell

The moment anyone stands up in front of a group of people, he or she is put in a vulnerable position. For children, from the moment they start school, the key person who can affirm their potential is the teacher – classmates may laugh at a poor presentation but the teacher, by affirming what has been well done (no matter how small that may be!) will give that child a positive self-esteem which will last through adult life.

There are always children who can test every boundary but affirmation can be instrumental in changing the direction a young life might be taking.

Presenting to a class provides a structured and boundaried context in which a child has to learn and demonstrate measurable skills. It also provides the *perfect context* for affirmation and constructive criticism which can build in the kind of confidence and good self-esteem which can change the culture of a nation.

I meet many people who found the worst thing they had to do at school was their presentation to the class. The combination of nervousness, vulnerability, relief and then disappointment when the presentation got a low mark – after putting in supreme effort – made the presentation session the equivalent of facing the guillotine! I should also say there are fantastic teachers who really work hard at making this a positive experience for the kids, giving affirmation, support and drawing the best out of the them – even when they have kids who won't prepare and make it obvious they've no interest in being anything other than the class dummy!

I'd like to look at some of the criteria teachers are given for using with children. Then I'll look at the same criteria from a different perspective which are aimed at achieving the same goals and at the same time build the kind of self-esteem and confidence that will be of lasting benefit for the kids.

The Fairy Godmother's checklist

Before Cinderella went to the ball, her fairy godmother had gone through a checklist of what she would need. Similarly pupils are given a checklist of what needs to be prepared for their talk and I've below is a sample list.

Planning your talk (sample)

- Choose a Topic
- Research for information (use books, computer, encyclopedias, magazines).
- Organize your material – take notes.
- Write the key points on key cards for prompts.
- Prepare visual aids, e.g. posters, objects, books etc.
- Learn your talk, know what you want to say but don't memorize it word for word.
- Talk on your subject for 3 minutes using your cards only, no script, no reading.

Think about your presentation

Clarity	- how clearly you speak, pauses, don't race
Projection	- how loud your voice should be so everyone can hear everything
Fluency	- don't falter or stop because you have forgotten
Purpose	- give lots of information and facts about your subject – consider the introduction and conclusion (these are important) – make it interesting and enjoyable for the listener
Questions	- be prepared to answer questions on the topic
Practice your talk	- be confident and don't forget to smile and enjoy yourself

This is a good checklist from an educational point of view. From the perspective of someone hearing speakers, both within their own businesses and at events, there are a couple of additional criteria which, when introduced at school level, will foster confidence, self-esteem and communication skills.

Cinderella's alternative checklist

I really appreciate there is a lot of material in the market about this subject so this is just my contribution.

1. It is always helpful for children to *work from their strengths rather than their weaknesses*. For example, if a child is a natural extrovert, then that can be used to develop skills in using humor in a talk. A natural introvert could use good quotes rather than jokes. By working from their strengths, they will usually identify their passion (see Chapter 3 Plates and Pebbles).

2. Too much research can lead to *verbal diarrhea*, unclear speech (as they try to get through all their material), and sometimes over-confidence. It is better to consider a few interesting pieces of information that can be used to help the presenter develop other skills, for example, storytelling, using visual aids etc

3. Skills required of a speaker (whatever age!):

Dealing with nerves: how to learn breathing techniques, visualizing something positive for after the event etc

Use of humor: gives the audience a feel-good factor and as long as the speaker has not lost control, even in the midst of lots of laughter, then that is a plus

Reading the audience: learning to tell when the listeners are bored and then having the skill to 'lift the game,' i.e. reengage the audience

Understanding self: so that they speak authentically – not trying to be something they are not

Verbal/non-verbal: learning to breath well so as to slow down the tendency to speak too quickly, eye contact, smiling, 'drama,' volume, use of tone etc, avoiding waffling – good research and content planning

Being fresh: being physically and mentally at your best for each talk – even though you're not necessarily feeling it!

Failure: learning from mistakes

'No pressure, no diamonds.'   Mary Case

Planning the talk

Key criteria:

- Good research
- Planned content – start, middle, ending
- Key cards for prompting
- Simple and effective props
- Work from your strengths
- Understanding the heart of the message rather than memorizing lots of words
- Relaxed, effective delivery to audience – interesting and enjoyable for both the speaker and the listener.
- Remember it's not the end of the world!

A case study

I initially became involved in working with schools when I had the enormous fun of helping a couple of 10-year olds prepare for a school talk. They had given a talk and felt they had done really well, only to discover their marks were very poor. What had happened was that during the talk on Roman feasts, they had mentioned that fish was stored in a stoppered vessel until it had decomposed into a liquid that became the fish sauce (don't kids just love the gruesome details!). At this point, someone in the class had laughed at the grossness of this, and the speakers had also laughed and then continued with the talk. They were marked down for laughing along with the member of the 'audience.' They knew they were due to give another talk but were quite discouraged about it and getting anxious.

I asked them to go through the talk they were preparing and present it to me as if it was in the classroom. We then spent some time going through a simplified version of the coaching material I use with adults. As kids usually are honest about themselves, it wasn't too difficult to get them to give their own critique about their planned talk. We then watched a couple of video clips of professional speakers with different styles and then they redid their talks. I then took their places and redid their talks exactly as they had presented them to me and got them to critique what I did. It was hilarious and when they then did their talks again, there was a vast improvement. I'm also delighted to say they got the top marks at their next presentation!

Understanding their strengths and weaknesses is key to the whole area of self-esteem and confidence. By strengths I mean *what are the things they really like about themselves and like doing*. Weaknesses are what they don't like about themselves or don't like doing. One child really likes her ability to swim well and it made her feel proud of herself. She wasn't happy with her friends liking her one minute and ignoring her the next, so she didn't like trying to make new friends. The other pupil loved dance and drama and her natural tendency would be to move about a bit and gesture with her arms and hands. She tried to be formal in her delivery style and felt bad about herself for failing to keep her body movements to a minimum. We spent time looking at allowing her natural body language to enhance her talk without it becoming distracting.

By talking through their strengths and weaknesses and giving them tools to deal with how they felt, the pupils started to understand what was going on internally and learned to react positively. They discovered their significance and gained a sense of self-respect and dignity. These are tools they can use for the rest of their lives.

In the school for rabbits, one rabbit was really great in the swimming pool but not too good at volleyball. One day he came to school and discovered that all but one period of swimming had been changed to volleyball so that he would get better at it. He stopped winning any swimming prizes and never made the volleyball team either!

The Gift of the Gab Prize

I run a four-stage confidence and communication skills program for schools to support and serve the teaching staff in what they are aiming to achieve, in terms of the school curriculum. By incorporating self-esteem and confidence-building elements into their normal program, communication and inter-personal skills develop too.

Stage One:	Nursery age – P2
Stage Two:	P6/7 Gift of the Gab prize
Stage Three:	13 – 15 year olds
Stage Four:	5/6 Year

The work involved for each stage involves is minimal but reinforces earlier work. The aim with the Gift of the Gab prize is that older kids will use their communication and delivery skills not just to win the prize but to coach younger kids down the school for their 'show and tell' times. Hopefully, most of the kids leaving school will have enough confidence to deal with whatever life throws at them.

How to develop the Gift of the Gab

1. Understanding self – we communicate out of who we are

- Strengths (what do you really like about yourself):
- Weaknesses (what don't you like doing):
- Passions (what do you enjoy most about life):
- Body Language (what signals do you give to other people to build relationships):
- Are you: Relaxed/self-conscious
  Eye contact/avoidance
  Embracing/distancing

2. Who would be in your favorite audience and why?

3. Giving the Presentation

Which do you enjoy most:

- the time preparing
- the talk
- the time afterwards?

Why?

4. What makes you nervous when you have to give a talk?

5. How would you rate the 'take-away' value of your talks?
(what the audience will remember long after the talk has finished)

Good, average or not a lot

The Talk

1. Write out how you normally plan your talks (what research do you do, what props do you use, how do you write it out?)

2, If you think about your favorite TV presenters, what do you like about how they present?

What don't you like?

Thinking of what you've just written, what would you like to include in your own style?

What would you like to avoid?

3. Content – this is the really important part.
    *   Start – what do you say that captures the audiences attention?

- Middle – what is the 'high' point (the information that really makes the audience interested)?

- Endings – what is the snappy finish (the audience would like to hear more)?

4. In which of the following area/s would you like to develop:

Content – beginnings, middles and endings

Communication skills i.e. use of words, humor, body language

Interaction with the audience i.e. eye contact, use of questions

Use of technical resources i.e. props

Reading the audience i.e. are they showing signs of being bored, getting out of control (talking to each other rather than listening)

<u>Some really useful tips</u>

1   Write key points on some cards and at the top put 'SLOW DOWN – BREATHE.' This will remind you not to rush your words and keep you relaxed.

2   The audience want to hear something interesting, not just a lot of facts, so think about what you are saying as if you were in the audience.

3   Keep the props simple so you don't end up forgetting what you want to say because the prop has broken down or got stuck.

4   To stay relaxed, focus your mind on something really nice that is happening after school – a favorite TV program, a club etc. When you get up to do your talk, remember that really nice thing that is happening and the talk won't seem such a big deal.

4   Remember you are the star and have something really good to say (so long as you've done your preparation well!). So enjoy yourself. However, don't be overconfident or you could come a cropper – remember the tortoise and the hare!

8

And Finally ...

The first manufactured golf balls were smooth, but then someone realized that if the surface was rough, they traveled much farther through the air. From then on, all the golf balls were dimpled. Rough spots can be the means of helping you develop as a speaker.

If you apply the principles of this book, whatever age or stage you are at, your game will improve.

Finally

- **Be realistic.** Only Robinson Crusoe had everything done by Friday!

- **Be yourself.** If it weren't for caffeine, some people would have no personality!

- **Do your homework.**
  'If there is no struggle, there is no progress.'
  Fred Douglass

- **Care for your audiences.**
  *'It is the part of a good shepherd to shear his flock,
  not to skin it.'*
  Latin proverb

- **Have fun.**
  *'He has achieved success who has lived well,
  laughed often, and loved much.'*
  Bessie Stanley

May you all be blessed

with fruitful words

and full lives.

Appendix 1 – Sample Feedback Sheet

FEEDBACK FORM

In an endeavor to consistently provide value during my seminars and keynotes/workshops, it is essential to listen to what the participants feel have benefited them most. Your answers to the following questions would be greatly appreciated.

Name   Company/Location   Position

_____   _____   _____

General Feedback	Please mark out of 10	Comments
Material Content*	1 2 3 4 5 6 7 8 9 10	_____
Presentation & Delivery	1 2 3 4 5 6 7 8 9 10	_____
Content of Speech	1 2 3 4 5 6 7 8 9 10	_____
Use & Effect of Humor	1 2 3 4 5 6 7 8 9 10	_____
Impact on Audience	1 2 3 4 5 6 7 8 9 10	_____
Value	1 2 3 4 5 6 7 8 9 10	_____

*Workshops

Specific Comments: Please highlight what has been most helpful for you. Are there any areas which you feel would benefit from follow-up courses?

_____

_____

_____

Percentage score you give the speaker (please circle):

10%   20%   30%   40%   50%   60%   70%   80%   90%   100%

And, finally, our service to you – how can we improve it?

Appendix 2

Sample Pre-Event Questionnaire

This aim of this questionnaire is to enable the speaker to tailor his or her presentation to the exact needs of your event. Feel free to skip over any answers which would merely duplicate answers to previous questions or which might be irrelevant due to the nature of this program. Your help will increase the value of this program to your audience! You may copy and paste this questionnaire into your word processing program, or we can deliver it to you. Please return the Pre-Event Questionnaire as soon as possible.

Pre-Event Questionnaire

I. YOUR EVENT

1. What is the meeting's theme?
2. What is the specific purpose of this meeting?
3. What type of meeting is it? (annual meeting, awards ceremony, sales kick-off, etc.)
4. Who (if anyone) is on the program just before the speaker and what is his/her presentation topic?
5. Who (if anyone) is on the program right after the speaker and what is his/her presentation topic?
6. Which company executives and/or industry experts will be speaking at this meeting?

II. THE PRESENTATION

1. What is the speaker's role in your program (opening or closing, keynote, breakout, etc.)?
2. What are the exact times for the speaker's presentation?
    Start Time: End Time:

Please send us a copy of the meeting program and agenda so he can see how his program fits in. Thank you!

3. How will most of the audience be dressed?

4. How will the executives be dressed?

5. How should the speaker be dressed? (suit and tie; sport coat and open collar shirt; slacks and shirt; other)

6. Who will be introducing the speaker to your group?

7. What is most important to you concerning the content of the speaker's program? (i.e. use of examples, exercises, handout, etc.)

8. What is most important to you in the working relationship with the speaker?

9. What themes/threads (other than the primary topic of the speaker's program) would you like to see woven into the program?

10. When your people leave the program, what three concepts/skills/ideas would you like them to have?

    1.

    2.

    3.

III. THE AUDIENCE

1. Number in the audience: Are spouses invited?

2. Male/female percentage: M   F

3. Average age group?   Range of age to

4 What industry sectors do they represent?

IV. BACKGROUND

1. What separates your high-achievers from the others?

2. What are some of the challenges your organization and your people/members face on a day-to-day basis?

3. What areas of challenge pose the greatest opportunity for improvement?

4. What are the most significant events that have occurred, and that have affected, your industry, organization, or group during the past year? (i.e. mergers, downsizing, etc.)

5. What is the primary product or service that you offer?

6. What are the two most important benefits you offer to your customers?

   A.

   B.

7. What are 2 or 3 achievements of which your organization is most proud?

V. LEARNING TOOLS

Most audiences want something to help them continue learning after the presentation has ended. What do you prefer?

- Customized workbook
- Books or Audio Tapes/CDs for the delegates
- Training Sessions to follow on from the speaker's sessions
- Visit the speaker's web site for more details

How do you wish to handle these?

- Purchase at quantity discount to distribute to participants at the event
- Offer learning materials to participants for purchase at the event.
- Let participants order the materials from the speaker after the presentation.

VI. LOGISTICAL INFORMATION

1. Hotel Name & Address

Phone:

Fax:

Email:

2. Hotel Confirmation Number:

3. Name of meeting room:

4. Into what airport should we schedule the speaker's flight?

5. How far is the hotel from the airport?

6. How should the speaker travel to the hotel? (take cab, rent car, driver will pick up, etc.)?

7. Would you like the speaker to notify someone after he/she arrives at the hotel? If so, whom shall he contact:

   Phone:

8. Contact at meeting site:

   Name: Title: Phone:

   On site arrival date:

9. Are there any pre-meeting engagements (i.e. breakfast or lunch)? If so, where and when are they scheduled:

MANY THANKS

Appendix 3 – Venue Checklist

1	The Room:	size
		temperature
		fresh air
2	Lighting:	appropriate for, e.g. PowerPoint
3	Seating:	is it right for what you're needing it for
4	Acoustics	
5	Platform:	lectern height
		hazards
6	Technical:	PowerPoint
		mikes
7	Contacts:	for technical issues
		for the main event
		other speakers
8	Pre-Speaking Routine:	
		walking the room
		imagine the audience
		imagine the applause

Appendix 4 – Travel bag

Travel bag Checklist (I know this is all common sense but this is a practical book after all!)

1. Technical: laptop (if necessary) and power cable

   PowerPoint presentation

   relevant props

   mobile phone charger

   spare batteries

2. Paperwork: Train/plane tickets

   Briefing paper and contact details

   Relevant correspondence

   Talk notes and prompt cards

   Receipts envelope

3. If overnight: toothbrush & toothpaste

   deodorant

   aftershave/perfume

   hairbrush

4. Just in case items: spare change of shirt/blouse, etc.

   shoe polish

Index

Index

Breinigsville, PA USA
06 July 2010
241252BV00003B/14/P